Greek Architecture

Roland Martin

Greek Architecture

E 6 3

Architecture of Crete, Greece, and the Greek World

Electa/*RIZZOLI* NEW YORK

Photographs: Bruno Balestrini
Layout: Arturo Anzani

Library of Congress Cataloging in Publication Data

Martin, Roland, 1912-
  Greek architecture

  (History of world architecture)
  Bibliography: p.
  Includes index.
  1. Architecture, Greek.   I. Title.   II. Series:
History of world architecture (Electa/Rizzoli)
NA270.M318   1988   722'.8   88-42689
ISBN 0-8478-0968-4 (pbk.)

Copyright ©1980 by
Electa S.p.A., Milan

Paperback edition first published
in the United States of America in 1988
by Rizzoli International Publications, Inc.
597 Fifth Avenue, New York, NY 10017

This volume is the redesigned paperback
of the original Italian edition published in 1972
by Electa S.p.A., Milan,
and the English edition published in 1974
by Harry N. Abrams, Inc., New York

Printed in Italy

TABLE OF CONTENTS

One hesitates to include a study of the architecture of Crete in a work devoted to Greek architecture, for one is uncertain of the bonds that can be established between two forms of monumental creation—each so different in spirit, in conception of mass and space, and in the use of decorative values. Would it not be better to combine the study of Cretan palatial architecture with that of Oriental palaces? The affinities are obvious, the plans and interiors undoubtedly similar. Nevertheless geographical connections, as well as historical ties and certain shared enduring principles, justify the present decision to treat both Greek and Cretan architecture within the covers of a single book. For the hiatus between the two is bridged by Mycenaean architecture—itself, as we now know, a Greek creation, the work of Greek-speaking peoples. In Mycenaean architecture Minoan forms and elements became integrated with structures indigenous to the mainland; and in the process of adaptation we will find a parallel, toward the close of our period, with transformations of Hellenistic architecture as it evolved toward the architecture of Rome.

Roman architecture is also an amalgam of diverse elements, some borrowed from the Greek tradition that supplied the forms, styles, and decoration, others derived from Italic structures developed by the extant civilizations of Italy. One can discern in it something of the unity that binds together the various periods and different moments of architectural creation in the Greek world during the first two millennia. Thus we begin this study with the formative stage of Minoan architecture, the period of the first palaces in the Middle Minoan era (about 2000–1900 B.C.). The different, and for our purposes largely irrelevant, forms of the Early Bronze Age, which pertain more directly to prehistory and the Neolithic epoch, have been deliberately omitted. In architecture the separation was quite abrupt, marked by the building of the early palaces which heralded a new world.

Similarly, on the mainland, our point of departure will be the Mycenaean works which, as a result of borrowings from Crete, profoundly modified the Helladic tradition in the fourteenth and thirteenth centuries. We shall be concerned only with the great moments of architectural creation that exerted a relative influence on the birth of truly Greek architecture during the Geometric period, in the course of the eighth century B.C.

It is my intention to interpret the great phases of architectural creation within their political, social, and religious context, in relation to the evolution of the human environment which conditions and explains the architectural evolution. Thus I have decided to distinguish only two great periods of Greek architecture. The first is a period of infancy and growth, of searching for plans and forms, of archaic exuberance and fecundity yielding gradually to the restraint and regulation of Classical discipline. This period lasted from the eighth to the fourth centuries B.C. The various aspects of its creative power are examined within their political or religious framework, with due allowance for the building methods and techniques peculiar to Greece.

The second period, called Hellenistic, corresponds to an architectural development encouraged and explained by profound political changes. While modifying and adapting classical forms and structures, Hellenistic architecture created a mode of expression whose evolution ends with Roman architecture and the Western world. Hellenistic architecture developed in a more restricted framework, that of the cities. The town-planning philosophy imposed upon various types of buildings—religious, civic, or private—the changes made necessary by the urban situation; this is the most characteristic element of the period, whose heritage was to be enjoyed for several centuries.

This manner of presentation seems to us to bring out more clearly the conditions and the originality of architectural creation in the Greek world than does the traditional dismemberment into chronological periods whose characteristics are largely external, less related to the actual societies as expressed in their monuments.

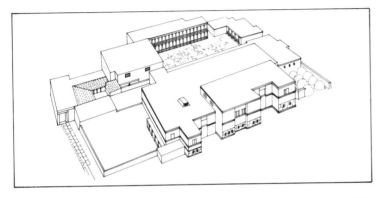

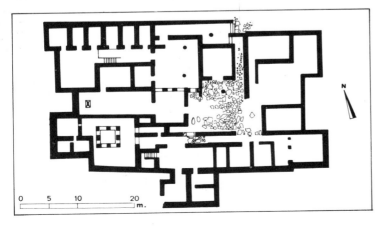

MINOAN CRETE

With its early place in time and with the originality of its inspiration, Minoan Crete marks the historical beginning of Western architecture.

In the great palaces of the Late Minoan era, between 1600 and 1400 B.C., one recognizes both the broad principles and the many refinements and subtleties of Cretan architecture in their most explicit form; it is a royal and palatial architecture of fine shades and hierarchical distinctions, combining spatial and decorative values in a balance achieved only by a few privileged periods of architectural history.

Recent excavations and detailed studies of the ruins and artifacts of the first palaces have made it possible to trace the source of this wave of creativity to the civilization of the Middle Minoan era (2000–1700 B.C.). What were the historical circumstances that enabled Crete to pull away from the rest of the Aegean world, to seize its own style, and to create the forms of a dynamic civilization? Crete, after 1600, rescued the lands along the Aegean shore from mediocrity, as each, in its turn, emerged from the simpler and more rigid forms of the Early and Middle Helladic civilizations. The writing in hieroglyphs that appeared about this time remains undeciphered. Only archaeology, with the measure of hypothesis that it possesses, can suggest certain aspects of the evolution that transformed a fragmented society, dispersed among villages or modest territorial units, into a more centralized political entity; princes, or priest-kings, assembled in their palaces the rudiments of an urban system and established a series of city-states, of which Mallia, Knossos, Zakro, and Palaikastro are the best-known examples. These priest-kings, exercising religious as well as political functions in their territories, doubtless formed the autonomous political groups whose resources were dependent on these zones, though apparently there were no rivalries fierce enough to require defensive organizations of any great strength. The kings could not equal the power of their neighbors, with whom, however, they maintained commercial and, no doubt, artistic contacts. In Egypt, the Pharaohs of the New Kingdom had restored the authority of Thebes and resumed their policy of northward expansion into Palestine and Syria, where Egyptian products mingled with those from Cretan cities. Through trading in these markets the Minoans became acquainted with a civilization in full renaissance whose painting offered a wealth of models and whose architecture had broken away from the severity and rigidity of the Old Kingdom by developing orders, introducing colonnades, and exploiting the majesty of the hypostyle hall. The Cretans were to feel the effects of this vigorous renaissance.

Along the eastern Mediterranean the Phoenician harbors of Byblos and Ugarit and the ports of call on Cyprus gave access to a network of interior routes that led ultimately to the great Babylonia of Hammurabi. Mari on the Euphrates, and Tell Atchana on the Orontes where it turns southwest toward the sea, were stops along the way, and must certainly have been

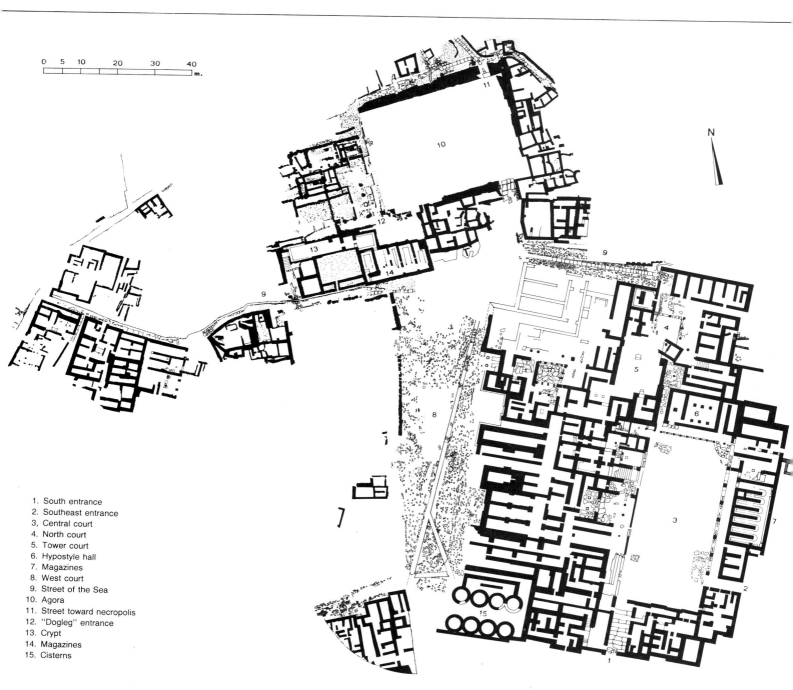

1. *Mallia, perspective reconstruction of palace, from northwest (from Graham, 1962).*

2. *Mallia, crypt rooms. Middle Minoan, c. 2000-1700 B.C.*

3. *Mallia, plan of House E (from Graham, 1962).*

4. *Mallia, plan of palace and northwest excavations. Middle Minoan 2000-1700 B.C., after Graham (1962).*

1. South entrance
2. Southeast entrance
3. Central court
4. North court
5. Tower court
6. Hypostyle hall
7. Magazines
8. West court
9. Street of the Sea
10. Agora
11. Street toward necropolis
12. "Dogleg" entrance
13. Crypt
14. Magazines
15. Cisterns

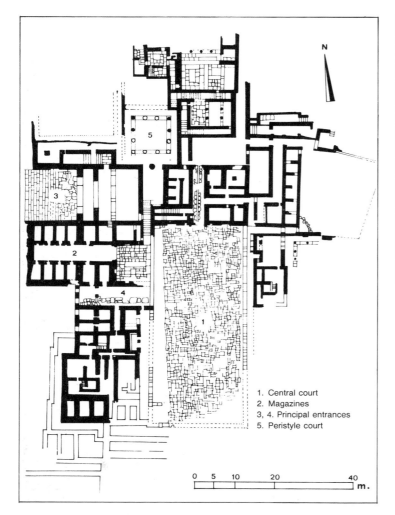

5. Phaistos, plan of second palace (from Graham, 1962).

1. Central court
2. Magazines
3, 4. Principal entrances
5. Peristyle court

0 5 10   20   40
━━━━━━━━━━━━━━━━━━━ m.

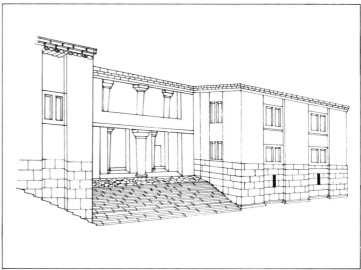

6. Phaistos, reconstruction of propylon (from Graham, 1962).

familiar to Minoan travelers. Thus Cretan expansion and the first great monuments of Minoan civilization occurred, in the early second millennium, at a time of flux and dynamic creativity in the territories with which Crete had contact; the Helladic civilizations, clinging more tenaciously to pre-Bronze Age trends, were left far behind. It was thanks to these contacts that the Cretans worked out the basic forms of their palace architecture. The full development came in the following period, under the enlightened domination of the princes of Knossos, who undoubtedly achieved the unification of Crete partly to their own advantage.

The palaces of Mallia, Zakro, and even Phaistos, if less sumptuous than Knossos, reveal more clearly the original features of this Old Palace architecture.

The First Palaces

The rectangular court is immediately recognizable as the key element, whose unifying role was to grow steadily more important (165 by 72 1/2 feet at Mallia; 165 by 82 1/2 feet at Knossos, where it is equally ancient). It is not the cellular unit seen in Oriental palaces—Mari, for example—a module around which surrounding rooms are organized, its contours reflected on the exterior walls of the complex; such units, repeated as often as required, form a loosely structured whole. By contrast the Minoan court has its own independent value and creates its own space; it derives its unifying influence from its role as a traffic hub and from the diversified rhythm of its facades, which reflect the diverse functions served by the "quarters" of the palace.

7. *Phaistos, theater and west court of palace, from northwest. c. 1700–1400 B.C.*

8. *Phaistos, west court of palace, from west. c. 1700-1400 B.C.*

9. *Phaistos, central court of palace, from south. c. 1700–1400 B.C.*
10. *Phaistos, magazines on central court of palace. c. 1700–1400 B.C.*

11. *Knossos, plan of palace (from Graham, 1962).*

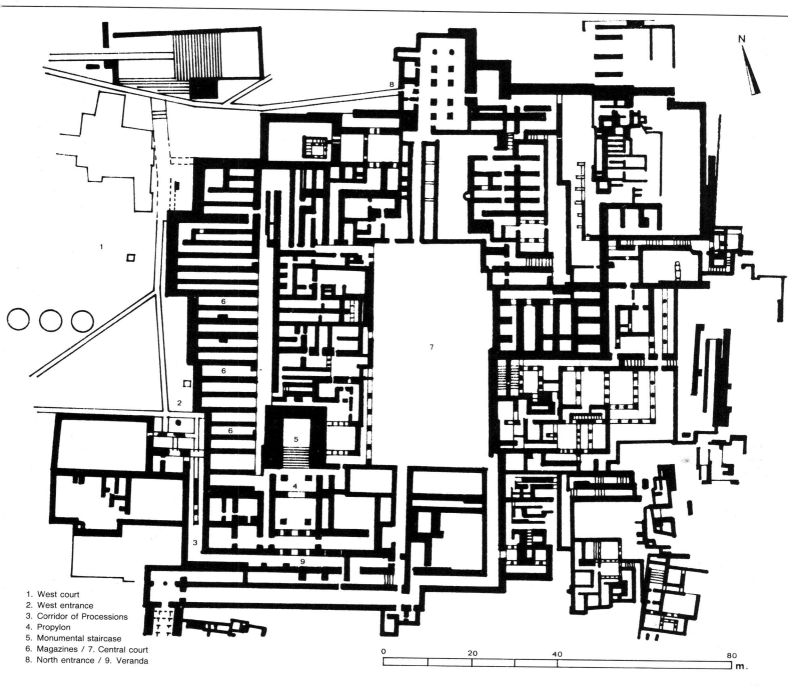

1. West court
2. West entrance
3. Corridor of Processions
4. Propylon
5. Monumental staircase
6. Magazines / 7. Central court
8. North entrance / 9. Veranda

*12. Knossos, western section of palace,
from north.*

*13. Knossos, south portico and
monumental staircase of palace.*

*14. Knossos, central court of palace,
facade of "throne room" (restored),
from east.*

At Mallia the disposition of the entrances seems to have remained more or less the same. The south and southeast entrances lead directly, through a vestibule and a passageway, into the central court. The approach from the north is more devious and may have undergone some modifications: from the so-called Street of the Sea one first entered a little court bordered by an L-shaped portico, from which one emerged into the great court by way of a paved vestibule and passageway. These skirt the western wall of an impressive triple-aisled hypostyle hall with two rows of three pillars, and the hall had access to the court through a dogleg passage incorporating a pillared vestibule.

As subsequently became the rule, the sides of the court were lined with porticoes or given some monumental treatment suitable to their function: at Mallia the east facade is distinguished by a long portico of square pillars alternating with circular columns. This portico borders a string of so-called magazines, rectangular storage rooms dating from the earliest phase of the palace's history. The treatment of the south facade is less refined: a long segmented wall on a massive plinth was pierced by wide bays intended to light a series of workshops. On the west, the monumentality of the facade reflects a change of function. Service quarters took up the east and south sides of the court, but the west side contained rooms of state having religious or administrative purposes. The heart of the official life of the palace appears to have been at the center of the west side, in two communicating rooms: a triple-aisled hall entered by two side doors, which may have been a "throne room," and, through a wide opening, another pillared room beyond. This central group was flanked by two important features: to the north a monumental staircase leading to the upper floor was bordered by a platform raised a few steps above the level of the court that it dominated. On the south a broad passage gave access to the great western magazines; further south another terrace bordered by several steps was doubtless in some way

15. Knossos, magazines on ground
floor in western section of palace, from
east.

16. Knossos, central court of palace,
west side.

17. Knossos, megaron above Hall of
Double Axes, east wing of palace,
from west.

connected with a slab for offerings, imbedded in the ground at the foot of the steps. Religious festivals and political life were closely associated within this architectural setting, a modest prelude to the future splendors of Knossos.

These ancient elements, scarcely modified in the course of the alterations and enlargements of the second palace at Mallia, are used to the same effect at Phaistos, on that splendid plateau that commands the Messara plain and the magnificent panoramic view of Mount Ida to the north. The access roads, the court, some of the magazines on the west, and the first few apartments to the southeast form part of the original structure. The over-all conception has crystallized. As at Mallia, the court presents a variety of facades: somewhat blank and rather less elegant toward the north and bordered on the east by a narrow portico with squat, crowded pillars. The west side was again reserved for administrative offices and rooms of state, which were remodeled as part of the second palace when the monumental entrance on the northwest and a portion of the esplanade were built over the razed areas of the first palace.

Thus, the principles of Minoan architecture were the work of the builders of the first great palaces: the distributional and centralizing role played by the court, which was treated as an autonomous primordial element; the functional principle that controlled the siting of the various quarters— political, administrative, religious, domestic—around the sides of the court; and the juxtaposition of private accommodations, rooms of state, magazines, and workshops. Certain architectural forms have already been assimilated: the use of the column and the pillar in alternation for the porticoes that line the courts; their function of support in subdividing the interior space of the halls; their decorative role in the loggias and baldachins of Mallia; the technique of using large slabs of *ammouda* (yellow limestone) at the base of the walls or for framing openings; the practical and monumental value of broad flights of steps.

The builders of the second palaces developed and extended these techniques and forms, eventually learning to handle them with a facility and ease that can be fully appreciated only in the palace of Knossos. It should not be forgotten, however, that these skills had been originally mastered by the Cretans of the first period, who, in turn, had borrowed them from the great neighboring civilizations of Egypt and Mesopotamia or Anatolia. The hypostyle hall at Mallia has been compared with Egyptian halls of the early New Kingdom; examples of the use of alternate columns and pillars are not unknown on the banks of the Nile. But any suggestion of a close relationship between the first Cretan palaces and the huge contemporary complexes of Mari or Mesopotamia must be treated with caution. If there seems to be a resemblance at first sight, an analysis of the construction principles and techniques reveals profound differences: the roles of the court have nothing in common; Mesopotamian facades are plainer and much more closed, and the column is used only for decoration; the plans of the halls

and living quarters are very different. The true kinship is more probably toward the north, with the architectures recently discovered at Tell Atchana and Beycesultan. Here the function of the court is the same: it articulates more flexibly the various parts of the palace, rather than being tied to a group of halls. The main court is bordered by porticoes and, as distinct from Mesopotamian practice, the column is used extensively to enlarge and animate the inside rooms. This is a more supple architecture, airier as well as more vivacious, and sharing with Minoan architecture its conception of the organization of space.

Before pursuing the development of these forms in the second palaces, we must pause to record another achievement of the Old Palace period, namely the elaboration of a genuine city system around the palace. Recent excavations over some ten years, particularly at Mallia, have revealed the broad outlines and even the precise details of a townscape with the palace as its principal feature.

A network of streets radiated from the palace in the direction of the sea and of the plain, toward the necropolises on the outskirts of the city. The system was not geometric but topographical and functional, reflecting the dwelling patterns of the earlier Bronze Age community. The general plan stressed the privileged situation of the palace and its approaches, but in addition the important role of the public square and its environs. The recent exploration and publication of this complex is a rich contribution to the urban history of Minoan Crete. The main square (96 by 132 feet), comparable in proportions to the central court of the palace, is surrounded on three sides, north, south, and east, by a high foundation wall (about three feet) of large slabs of *ammouda*. Varying in thickness from six to nearly eleven

23. Knossos, south house and, above, portion of entrance corridor to palace, from southwest.

24. Knossos, south portico of palace and "horns of consecration," from east.

feet, this wall perhaps supported the tiers of seats for a place of assembly similar to those that existed in the cities of archaic Crete, at Lato and Dreros. On the west, buildings not yet identified ended near the southwest corner in a little L-shaped portico. Behind the south foundation wall extended a complex of rooms treated as cellars that form a crypt reached by a few steps. These rooms communicated toward the east with a group of rectangular magazines, very carefully built and similar to those in the palace. The stuccoed walls, several times restored, and the presence of a column in the first chamber suggest that these are the remains of a building of studied monumentality whose crypt must have counted as a floor, on the same level as the small rooms lined up behind the south foundation wall of the court. Comparable in structure to the numerous crypts known in the Minoan palaces, the crypt at Mallia does not seem, to judge from the artifacts found among the excavations, to have had the religious basis attributed to the former examples. Its relations with the adjoining square, itself treated as an agora, and with the palace justify its discoverers in assigning to it a public role.

The ensemble in any case reveals the presence in the Minoan city of a center of public life, freely accessible to the citizens and close to the palace but quite independent of it. This undoubtedly reflects a political organization less centralized and less hierarchical than originally supposed.

The pottery and the study of successive layers of stucco and of construction details, as well as the later stages of development of the site, leave no uncertainty about the chronology of this crypt-square complex. It was laid out in Middle Minoan I and used until Late Minoan I or II; it appears then to have been encroached upon by other buildings, as if a change in political power had concentrated public life around the palace.

The Second Palaces

After 1700 the palace sites became the focus of power and authority which lasted through the sixteenth and fifteenth centuries. It led to a remarkable architectural development in the palaces and in their surroundings. Mallia dominated eastern Crete; Knossos and Phaistos, central Crete; Knossos may have exercised suzerainty even over the other regions. This is the time that the public square at Mallia and its adjoining structures fell into decay, whereas the palace was enlarged—a fairly obvious sign of some socio-political transformation, since the city itself continued to develop and spread, as did the city around the great palace of Knossos. The population of Knossos has been estimated at about 100,000, including those in the central quarters clustered around the palace, in the prosperous homes in the valleys bordering the paved roads, and the population of the port on the present site of Herakleion. This was an important capital, the center of a civilization whose radiance was to arouse the stagnant Aegean lands still in thrall to the civilizations of the Early and Middle Helladic eras, among which Mycenae was the most brilliant.

It would be tedious to describe in detail the great palaces of this period and the rich dwellings that surrounded them. The facts are readily available in specialized accounts. Our object is better served by concentrating upon the broad outlines and original features of New Palace architecture, illustrating our theme with examples drawn from various sites, notably Knossos, the most sumptuous. There are a few great principles that inspired the Cretan architect: a functional and organic composition, without concern for artificial bounds or symmetry, the use of the column, in isolation or to form a portico; the skillful and sometimes elaborate organization of volumes and interior spaces; a pronounced taste for linear and decorative structures, with a broad reliance on polychromy and mural painting. These buildings, palaces, and villas gave integrated expression to every aspect of public, religious, and private life.

Functional and Organic Composition

The first impression received by a visitor to the site of a Minoan palace is one of disorder, confusion, and a jumble of multiple elements unrestrained by any formal discipline. This impression comes from the agglomerative system of construction and the absence of a unified facade. The palace of Knossos covers a rectangle measuring approximately 495 feet east to west by 330 feet north to south. The contours are uncertain and only on the west is there a regular facade. The living quarters and workshop blocks simply cluster together, forming setbacks and salients. The entrances themselves project, on the south (great staircase gallery), or are recessed, on the west.

There are no right angles or continuous straight lines; instead there is a sinuous movement of projections and recessions that is interrupted only along the western esplanade, where the great paved streets terminate, by a massive plinth composed of alabaster orthostats, large vertical slabs some

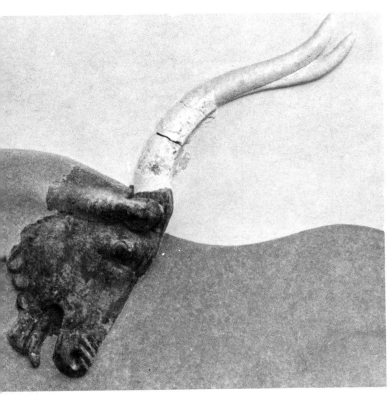

27. "Bull's Head," painted relief from north portico, Palace of Knossos. Herakleion, Museum.

28. "Blue Girls," fresco from Palace of Knossos. Herakleion, Museum.

three feet high. These rest on a projecting step, and above it once rose a wall of dressed stone; the second story was pierced with openings, square windows framed in wood, but the first story was perfectly blank. This bleakness was doubtless tempered by the timbers used to stiffen the masonry of rubble bedded in clay (some partitions were made of unbaked brick supported by wooden framing). This wall formed one side of a row of magazines opening on a north-south service passage, the masonry being sufficiently thick to carry the weight of the upper floors.

A similar sophistication is displayed at Phaistos: the Minoan architect was not insensitive to the monumental quality of an entrance facade and here exploited the remains of the first palace, which had been razed to the level of the orthostats at the base of the walls. The site was filled in and thick walls were built that enclose the magazines and enframe the propylon, set back to enlarge the esplanade which dominated, on the north, the broad steps reserved for spectators at public festivals. These steps abutted a handsome ashlar wall which formed the underpinning of another terrace. Here, as at Knossos, even the ups and downs of the site do not impose any regularity on the external contours of the palace; on the contrary, variations were cleverly exploited as terraces or platforms for the buildings annexed to the central core around the court.

In fact, the location and role of the central court provide the only unifying principle of the composition, but this unity is purely functional and makes no concessions to any demand of symmetry or axiality. It is based on the relations and lines of communication which unite the various quarters of the palace; it is physically realized in the long corridors into which the visitor to the palace is immediately plunged. At Knossos there is the famous Corridor of Processions, so named after the subject of its decorative frescoes. It starts from the innermost corner of the west porch, entered through either of two openings separated by a central column. After running for about 90 feet due south, between walls decorated by the procession of gift-bearers, it turns east and continues in that direction for another 148 feet; near the center of this stretch opens the landing and propylon of a great monumental staircase giving access to the rooms of state that occupied a large part of the upper floor of the west wing. The corridor next swings back north until it reaches the central court. This last change of direction created a sort of crossroads where also arrived the flow of traffic coming from the south by way of the monumental stairway known as the "stepped porch." This was actually a stepped causeway or viaduct treated as a portico; starting from the bottom of the valley, it reached in terraces to a level just below the south front of the palace and ran parallel to the Corridor of Processions. Another entrance, on the north, was also developed as an ascending corridor, which, after skirting a colonnaded gallery with stucco decorations, emerged almost on the axis of the central court.

These passages and corridors separate groups of rooms having different functions. At Knossos, as at Mallia, Phaistos, and Zakro, the places of

assembly and of worship, the audience chambers, and perhaps the administrative offices were ranged on two or three levels along the west side of the court. Their public character was expressed by a series of porticoes, and monumental staircases punctuated by vestibules with single or triple columns supporting in unequal rhythm the balconies and loggias of the upper floors. In these colorful, animated facades, developed on successive levels, motifs were freely juxtaposed with no attempt at imposing an artificial unity; their articulation reflected the diversity of the rooms within, and their functions. As we saw at Mallia and Phaistos, only the irregularities and setbacks of the domestic quarters and workshops, on the south and east, were sometimes disguised by an aligned colonnade forming a shallow portico.

One last feature of these compositions has particular appeal for the modern student of architecture: linked with movement and currents of circulation, it is never closed upon itself. At every instant it opens on the outdoors by a knowing use of porticoes and loggias disclosing neatly framed glimpses of the countryside. The best examples are found at Knossos, on the west, where the domestic apartments and the "Cretan magazines" are bordered with terraces and loggias; it is the same at Phaistos, on the north and east. The treatment of the porticoed rooms, arranging for a progressive opening from the interior light well to the unroofed terrace, creates an agreeable rapport between the building and the surrounding landscape. Sometimes the relationship is even more subtle. Thus the so-called Caravanserai, in the valley south of the palace of Knossos, was organized around a main hall with a colonnade broadly open to the north; the view toward the terraced pile of the palace, clinging to the sides of the hill, offered a picturesque and lively prospect. The refined sense of pictorial decoration, which we will discuss shortly, leaves little doubt that these effects were consciously sought.

Columns, Pillars, and Porticoes

Flexibility and movement make the originality of Minoan composition, and these find a particularly appropriate means of expression in columned and pillared structures. Since the early palaces the attraction of columned porticoes and facades, and of arrangements of pillars, is apparent.

The columnar motif occurs at the very entrance to the palace—the west propylon at Knossos and at Phaistos, and the entrances to the Little Palace of Knossos—and again with numerous variations inside, especially at Mallia and Knossos. Rooms of state or formal staircases to that level have a median column that divides the passageway in two. Moreover, there are many rooms with one or more columns, at basement level as well as on the various upper floors. Much more subtle and refined are the effects achieved with porticoes or by using pillars as internal partitions. These are the characteristic features of the "Cretan megaron," best exemplified in the large palace at Knossos and the Little Palace, and at Phaistos. The Hall of the Double Axes in the

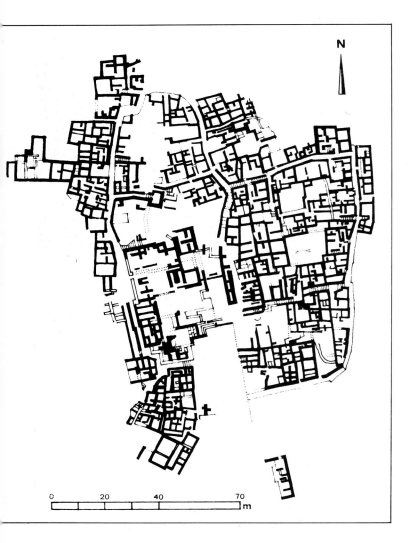

0   20   40   70
m

residential quarter of the Palace of Minos is a structure of this type. Illuminated from a light well on the west side through a triple opening formed by two columns, the principal room is divided by three rectangular pillars designed to receive a movable partition; the eastern half of the room is bordered by an L-shaped arrangement of pillars, three along the east, two along the south, pivoting on a massive corner pillar. Finally, the space beyond, similarly treated, is separated from the open terrace by an L-shaped portico with three columns along each leg and a stout corner pillar. The Little Palace offers a most appealing variation on the same theme. The megaron is at right angles to the outside walls; the two parts of the great hall, again separated by three rectangular pillars and a movable partition, are lit through columned openings by a lateral light well. Access to the hall is through a peristyle court with a small triple-column portico on all four sides, and the composition is continued on the axis by another pillared hall illuminated by a light well at the side. The agreeable charms of rhythmically filtered light combined with cunningly controlled ventilation can be readily appreciated.

The use of the interior peristyle court, admitting light and air into otherwise somewhat crowded spaces, was common in Cretan houses and villas. The architects of Phaistos made frequent use of it, especially on the north side, where porticoes continue the rhythm of the central court and smooth the transition to the north megaron with its view of the majestic slopes of Mount Ida.

Columns and pillars were also combined within single porticoes. At Mallia and Phaistos they border certain parts of the central court; in both palaces they are associated with the northern approaches. At Knossos, the portico along the north entrance had a more monumental function; with its double aisle, it became a veritable picture gallery sheltering a relief fresco of a charging bull.

In the villa of Hagia Triada, not far from Phaistos, the portico became an independent building opening onto an esplanade and concealing a row of small rooms, a sort of prototype of the chambered porticoes variously utilized by Greek cities in later centuries.

Finally must be mentioned the pleasing effect of the short columns placed on the substructure accompanying the flights of the stairwells. Two splendid examples are to be found at Knossos. To the east of the central court the residential quarter spreads over the face of the hill on five different levels, two of them no doubt higher than the court, one at the same level, and two lower. A great staircase, with two flights per floor, extended between landings around a light well pierced by columned openings. Traditional wooden columns, thinner at the bottom than at the top and crowned by thick cushion capitals, were found in place, heavily charred; plaster casts were promptly made and the restoration carried out in painted cement. The south "stepped porch" at Knossos, discussed above, was treated in exactly the same way—as a covered stairway whose roof was supported by a double row of columns resting on the low side walls; thus, along the entire stretch of nearly 300 feet it was possible to enjoy a broad view of the countryside and the successive projections of the south front of the palace.

Organization of Volumes and Interior Spaces

A corollary of the agglomerative plan was the diversified treatment of the different parts of the palace. The result was a rather sharp disparity between masses and levels, tending to create a first impression of somewhat anarchical congestion. No doubt this impression has some measure of validity for the peripheral areas of the palace. But to the extent that the excavations make possible a reliable reconstruction of the elevations, one can now glimpse some of the means employed to avoid an effect of harsh disparity.

The Minoan architect did not hesitate to use on occasion solid masses and blank surfaces: among such examples are the west facade of the palace of Knossos, the south side of the court at Mallia, and the north side of the court at Phaistos. These are massive structures on base courses of orthostats, enlivened only by a few jogs in the line of the wall and, no doubt, the wood-framed openings.

The play of diversified and animated facades is to be seen in full refinement in the monumental structures that lined the west sides of the great courts at Phaistos, Mallia, and Knossos. The rhythm in this case is very different, and the composition depends on the alternation of solids and voids at the various levels created by terraces and loggias, arranged above the ramps of formal staircases. At Phaistos the northern part of the west wall is developed in a series of alternating pillars and columns that opens on a wide room divided in two by a pair of central columns; beyond this an opening with pillars and columns gives access to a long corridor leading to the dimly lit magazines. This dynamic stretch of facade was followed, it seems, by flat surfaces whose details are still obscure. The same arrangement is found at Mallia, but there the levels make a further diversity. The central section of the facade was plain, edged by a long wall setting apart the great "throne room." At either end, however, there were voids: on the north were two series of steps, one defining a platform with a single central pillar, the other forming a staircase, doubtless leading to the upper floor; on the south, terracing aligned with the flat wall occupied the space left free by the setback of the rooms in the southwest corner.

At Knossos the skill of the architects found its boldest expression. Along the straight front a double rhythm of pillars is developed on each side of the principal element giving access to the throne room and the small sanctuaries: facades with a single pillar contained between two massive antae. To the south, the pillars form a regular border to conceal various projections and ill-related passages; to the north, the rhythm is enlivened by incorporating them in staircases, first a single pillar, then a group of three, all resting on intermediate steps. Moreover, the idiosyncrasies now discernible at the ground-floor level were accentuated in the second story

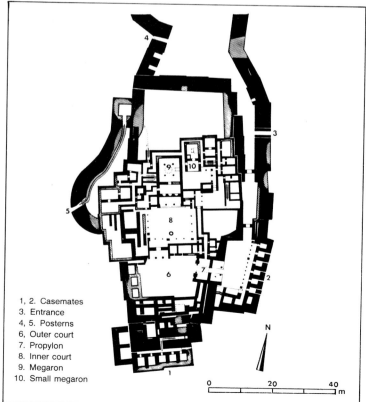

1, 2. Casemates
3. Entrance
4, 5. Posterns
6. Outer court
7. Propylon
8. Inner court
9. Megaron
10. Small megaron

N

0   20   40
                m

by a succession of balconies, simple windows, and loggias. This was a true pictorial architecture, whose attraction lay in the skillful manipulation of solids and voids that created contrasts of light and shade, and in the correspondence of horizontal and vertical planes.

The planning of the interior spaces indicates equal skill. We have already cited the plan of the "Cretan megaron" and the subtly graded transitions from the outdoor light to the diffused luminosity of the light well. The great staircase on the east side of the court can justly claim to be the finest example of this art. Its successive flights, adorned with columns, unfold around a light well, the sides opposite the flights bordered by loggias from which run corridors serving the dwelling apartments on each floor. An astonishing impression of balance, freedom, even subtlety and boldness results from a rhythm artfully mastered, wholly inspired by the movement that animates the composition, whose charm comes not so much from the ampleness of the volumes as from the elegance of the design.

Decorative Values, Polychromy, Murals

Although the Minoan architect did not overlook the arrangement of volumes and the subtle art of treating interior spaces harmoniously, his special domain was for linear and pictorial composition. The very technique of building and the nature of the materials favored the development of a taste for polychromy. The timbering that stiffened the stone and clay construction; the foundation walls of big well-mortared limestone slabs; the geometric wooden framing of the doors and windows; the play of pillars and columns, likewise in wood; the angular contours of the facades and terrace roofs, at various levels because of the juxtaposition of blocks of different height—all these suggest a feeling for contrast, polychromy, and pictorial effects. Since the period of the first palaces, perhaps under the influence of Egyptian painting, colors applied to plaster had enlivened the interiors, but the great frescoes were not made before 1600 B.C.

The frescoes at Knossos, like the architecture they complement, are vivacious and rich in movement. Columns, pillars, beams, lintels and jambs, all made of wood picked out with paint, formed the framework of the pictorial decoration. Brown or red backgrounds, as in the stairway and the corridor of the Hall of the Double Axes, brought out the ornamental motifs, in particular the great figure-eight shields. A characteristic feature of this decoration, so well adapted to the architectural lines, is the absence of corner limitations. The corners are, in fact, obliterated so as not to interrupt the movement, which appears to keep pace with the observer as he advances. An example is the great Procession Fresco in the long corridor leading from the west porch. As usual, the figured scenes are treated as a frieze, here a double frieze; the procession of gift-bearers keeps step with the visitor's progress from the door to the great south staircase. The forward motion is sustained, as it were, by a central undulating band of blue, drawn at mid-height just above or below the top of the men's loincloths; these are colored yellow, to contrast with the reddish tints of the flesh. These undulating lines turn the corners without interruption, thus creating unity of movement among the figures in the frieze. The frieze itself unfolds together with the interior space.

Other frescoes, such as those portraying crowds of men and women gathered on steps framed by architectural decoration to witness a religious ceremony or public games, carry into the palace eddies from a gay and colorful life; the rustling of skirts, the echo of shouts, and the hum of conversation are almost audible in these scenes, where unity and continuity of movement are suggested by the diversity of the attitudes, the heads and bodies turned in all directions, and the typically Mediterranean gesticulations. The general admiration aroused by the fresco called "La Parisienne" when it was first discovered about 1900, is well known.

Architectural composition was preoccupied with the problem of integrating the interior with the landscape outside. The same preoccupation is reflected in the frescoes at Amnisos and the landscape scenes at Knossos, with a blue bird swooping among the flowers of a rock garden, blue monkeys in a charmingly whimsical landscape, or evocations of a marine world. These paintings open up and brighten the inside rooms. Many centuries later, in the villas of Pompeii, landscapes were to supplement the gardens and peristyles by dissolving their walls and leading the eye beyond, toward broader horizons.

Of course, one should not overlook the hieratic and more restrictive scenes that decorate the so-called throne room at Knossos; more probably this room was a place of worship, with a chair for the priest tucked away in the dimness of the pillared vestibules behind the sanctuary—whose facade has been convincingly restored as the central motif of the west side of the great court. Even these scenes, slower paced but still far from static, are well adapted to the function and structure of the room. More sharply delimited

36. Mycenae, Lion Gate.

than the friezes, the paintings are also inseparable from the architecture.

Both are closely united in the same conception of space. They divide and animate space, release it from all restrictions, free it to respond to the dynamism of life, modulate it, soften and sharpen it to provide a setting for a society in which both men and women appear to have led full and joyous lives.

MYCENAEAN ARCHITECTURE

Toward 1400 B.C. the Cretan mode of life seems to have come to an end, or at least to have grown increasingly somber and muted. The Minoan heritage had already been partly assimilated by the mainland population; these mainland people were Greeks, as their recently deciphered language plainly shows. Their civilization flourished in the Peloponnese and, more especially, in the Argolid, where Mycenae became the center of the civilization and gave it its name.

For the visitor fresh from Crete who arrives before the Lion Gate at Mycenae, or threads his way through the fortified passages that guard the entrance to the palace of Tiryns, the impression of a new world is immediate and acute. This architecture is of a very different order, even though, once inside the walls, he discovers forms and elements that recall the Cretan palaces. But Minoan fluidity and dispersion have given way to concentration; spaces are tightly circumscribed by mighty perimeter walls with their bastions, curtains, constructed approaches, and heavily fortified gates protecting against any surprise attack. This is an architecture of conquering soldier kings, feudal overlords occupying dominant positions that have contours filled not with the ingeniously terraced, invitingly open apartments of Knossos, but by thick walls built of cyclopean blocks, barely hewn yet cunningly assembled. These walls are pierced by occasional posterns at the foot of fortified stairs or "casemates," like those at Tiryns, whose vaults of corbeled arches, closed at the top by two blocks leaning one against the other, have withstood the passage of the centuries. The gates are set back within these walls, and defensive works jut out to dominate the approaches and outflank the besieger. The doorway is framed by monolithic pillars; at Mycenae, the lintel of the Lion Gate is still in place and supports the famous ten-foot-high relief that fills the triangle of the relieving arch required by so great a span. The two lions, confronting from either side a column with capital and crown, assured the religious protection of the citadel.

Inside the citadel the buildings were grouped around the palace, itself reduced to a few rooms surrounding the megaron. At Mycenae the palace clung to a crumbling terrace: it is Tiryns, on its platform only eighty-six feet above the plain of Nauplia and Argos, that offers the best example of Mycenaean palace construction.

This is not to overlook the importance of the palace at Pylos, the remains

of the fortification of Athens, the still uncertain traces of the palace at Thebes, the fortifications of Gla in Boeotia, or the ruins of Malthi. Nonetheless, one always returns to Tiryns, whose plan, developed in the thirteenth century B.C. with remarkable unity of conception, reads like a working drawing. From the east entrance (the only one, except for a few posterns) leads a long ramp, twice interrupted by intermediate gates, toward the southern tip of the knoll; there, through a gate flanked by guardhouses, one enters the first court. This esplanade was surrounded by defense works on several levels, including casemates commanding the approach to the foot of the wall on the east and south. On the north side of the court opens a columnar propylon, already more Greek than Minoan with its two double-columned porticoes back-to-back on the central wall; the visitor then enters the main court porticoed on the east, west, and south sides, the north side being occupied by the facade of the megaron, the principal element of the palace around which the suites of domestic apartments were clustered. Very different from the Cretan megaron, the rectangular Mycenaean hall is entirely enclosed and preceded by a double vestibule; the first is an outer vestibule with two columns in antis, the inner one gives access through a single central door to the principal area. This span, in accordance with tradition, was occupied by a central hearth and four columns arranged in a square supporting the clerestory lantern that rose above the terrace roof. The wall frescoes here, with their essentially military themes, and the floors and stuccowork recall Minoan decoration and techniques. Although, compared to the Minoans, the Mycenaeans knew much more about large-scale stone work, both in polygonal blocks with rough-hewn faces and rectangular blocks laid in regular courses (as we will see in the tholos tombs), they also used the Minoan masonry of rubble bedded in clay, stiffened by horizontal and vertical timbers. This method involved plaster and stucco, and the Mycenaeans had quickly acquired the Cretan art of fresco. The porticoes, columned propylons, vestibules, and decorative techniques may have been derived from the Cretan repertory, but the principles of construction remained firmly within the mainland tradition. The centralizing role of the megaron is particularly conspicuous at Pylos; the mass of the megaron is detached by the lateral corridors that link it with the smaller rooms on either side. The court itself is an annex of the megaron, intended merely to free the approaches and display the facade; unlike the Cretan court, it has no structural function. The result is a progressive, hierarchic composition organized around the megaron, with a concern for monumentality and privileged areas that is foreign to Minoan architecture.

The taste for the monumental is expressed with special force in the tholos tombs of Mycenae, the most successful example of which is the so-called Treasury of Atreus. A long open-air passage or "dromos," carved out of the hillside, forms an entranceway 116 feet long and 20 feet wide between walls built of uniform blocks perfectly dressed and carefully laid. At the end

of this passage rises the facade of the tholos, flanked by half columns of green stone more than thirty-three feet high and decorated with spiral and chevron motifs. The door is monumental—nearly eighteen feet high and nine feet wide—and crowned by a monolithic lintel that occupies the entire width and depth of the opening. The relieving triangle above repeats the spiral motif on the columns around the door. The interior of the chamber is profoundly impressive. Circular in plan with a diameter of nearly fifty feet, the corbeled vault rises forty-five feet in thirty-three anglar courses of regular blocks, cut to a smooth curve of perfect elegance. Rarely have art, technique, and proportions been combined in such complete harmony.

During the fourteenth and thirteenth centuries many regions of the Mediterranean world received the impress of Mycenaean culture. But violent upheavals, touched off either by new waves of Hellenic migration—the Dorian invasion—or, as now seems more likely, by a series of revolts, were soon to bring about the downfall of Mycenae and obliterate its name from the map of the civilized world. The power and vigor of its architecture and the dynamism of its expansion, faint echoes of which still linger in Homeric poetry, must have had their effect on the birth of Greek art. This point is still debated, and it is not easy to determine the precise contribution of the Mycenaean heritage in the progressive inventions of early Greek architecture, to which we now must turn, passing over several centuries, notably the eleventh and tenth, that remain shrouded in obscurity.

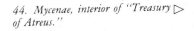

44. *Mycenae, interior of "Treasury* ▷
of Atreus."

45. Dreros (Crete), diagrammatic reconstruction of a temple (from Demargne, 1964).

46. Argos, terra cotta model of temple, from Sanctuary of Hera. Athens, National Museum.

From one end to the other of the Mediterranean regions that later formed the "Greek world," the collapse of Mycenaean civilization provoked migratory movements of people who were either simply drawn into the vacuum or driven by difficulties, external and internal, from one shore of the Aegean to the other. Dorian invasions from the north, Achaean movements, and Ionian migrations allowed few areas to escape these upheavals, and were hardly favorable to artistic and, in particular, architectural creation. Only the useful arts, especially ceramics, enable us to trace the threads that run through this Dark Age during which, from the eleventh to the eighth centuries B.C., the Greek peoples sought a new equilibrium and tested the political and social structures that were to result in the formation of the *polis,* the Greek city-state, an original and fruitful institution that fostered the most expressive forms of Greek art and architecture.

As evoked in the last books of the *Odyssey* and the poems of Hesiod, this social and political community was precariously based on an often uneasy partnership between clan structures and embryonic social groupings founded on common interests, between the landed aristocracy and the little men, tenant farmers, or smallholders. In this society political rights depended on property and family connections.

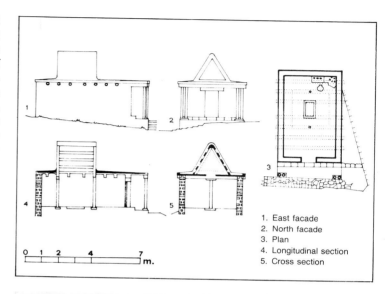

1. East facade
2. North facade
3. Plan
4. Longitudinal section
5. Cross section

0 1 2 4 7 m.

ORIGINS

The architecture first generated by these communities was merely practical and utilitarian, with no pretensions to monumentality; the abode of the gods was cast in the image of the abode of men.

This architecture retained nothing of the Mycenaean palatial tradition. A few isolated examples or more extensive sites such as ancient Smyrna account for our knowledge of the early forms of this renaissance. Each structure was separate and independent. Typically a house had only one room; this was first elliptical, then rectangular, later apsidal in plan. At Old Smyrna, the first two types are the oldest (eleventh to ninth century), the third was contemporary with the last Geometric period (end of ninth to first half of eighth century). Eighteen to twenty-three feet in length, in width eleven and one-half to thirteen feet at the most, these houses were made of sun-dried brick or rammed clay on a foundation of stones or rubble. Very soon these foundations became more important and were built of hewn blocks, then of orthostats, the large slabs set on edge that continue to be used throughout Greek architectural history. Wood posts on the inside, aligned on the principal axis, supported a rudimentary structure of ridge pole and branching lateral elements.

The roof was double-hipped, translated into stone in the manner of the little votive building on Samos. At Smyrna, as in the little Temple of Apollo Daphnephoros recently discovered at Eretria, the interior posts are

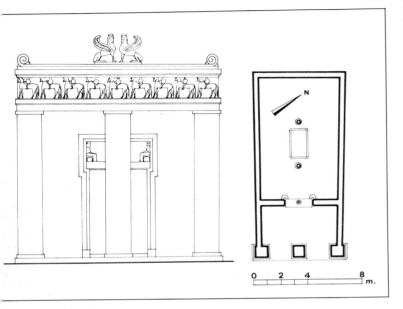

47. *Prinias, reconstruction of front elevation and plan, Temple A (from Charbonneaux-Martin-Villard, 1968).*

48. *Prinias, lintel of Temple A. Herakleion, Museum.*

49. *Thermon, plan of successive buildings of Temple of Apollo (from Charbonneaux-Martin-Villard, 1968).*

50. *Samos, plan of Sanctuary of Hera (from Bervé-Gruben, 1962).*

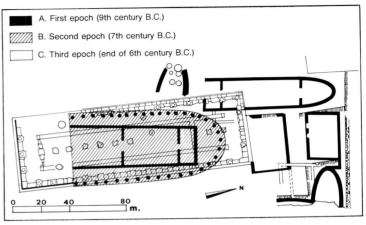

A. First epoch (9th century B.C.)
B. Second epoch (7th century B.C.)
C. Third epoch (end of 6th century B.C.)

0   20   40   80
m.

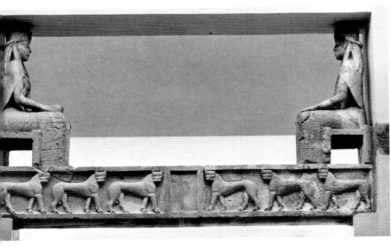

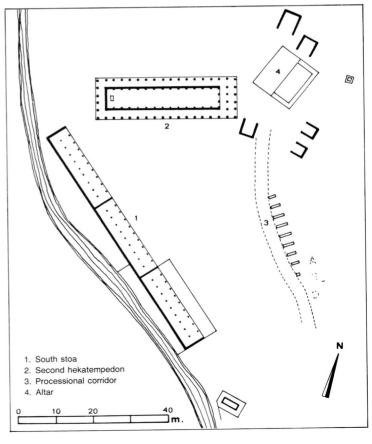

1. South stoa
2. Second hekatempedon
3. Processional corridor
4. Altar

0   10   20   40
m.

I. Knossos, palace.

II. Hagia Triada, one of the small staircases leading from the agora to the upper courtyard.

51. Samos, plan of Temple of Hera III, by Rhoikos and Theodoros (from Bervé-Gruben, 1962).

52. Samos, plan of Temple of Hera IV, by Polycrates of Samos (from Bervé-Gruben, 1962).

53. Eretria, plan of first Temple of Apollo Daphnephoros (from Auberson, 1968).

54. Larissa, Aeolic capital. Istanbul, Archaeological Museum.

55. Neandria, Aeolic capital. Istanbul, Archaeological Museum.

56. Delphi, Sanctuary of Apollo, reconstruction of front elevations of treasuries of Cnidos, Marseilles, and Siphnos (from Charbonneaux-Martin-Villard, 1968).

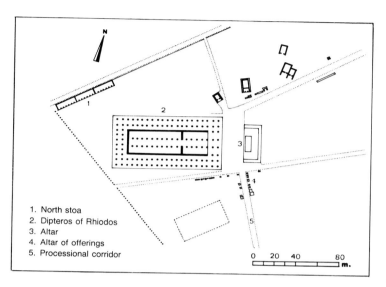

1. North stoa
2. Dipteros of Rhiodos
3. Altar
4. Altar of offerings
5. Processional corridor

0   20   40   80
m.

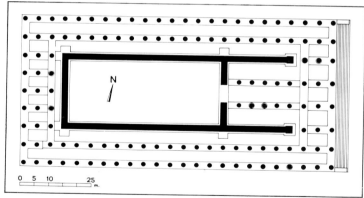

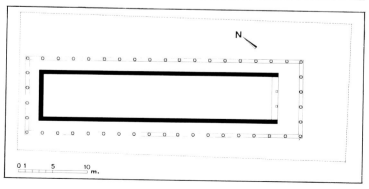

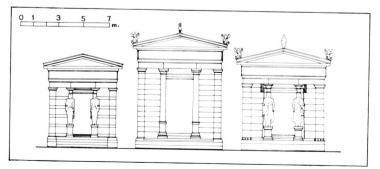

57. Delphi, Sanctuary of Apollo,
caryatid from Treasury of the
Siphnians. Delphi, Museum.

58. Delphi, Sanctuary of Apollo,
frieze (detail) from Treasury of the
Siphnians. Delphi, Museum.

asymmetrically distributed. There is a single post at one end, a double post at the other; it may be assumed that this double post supported a beam that received a heavier load because it carried the radial framing that reinforced the hip, whereas at the other end, corresponding to the facade, the pitched roof ended in a gable with a triangular pediment. Here again temple models in terra cotta from Perachora and Argos suggest and justify this reconstruction. Traces of the same system are to be found as late as the sixth century in the treasury of the Heraion at the mouth of the Sele River near Paestum (Greek Poseidonia).

The origin of the triangular pediment, often associated with an opening that lit and made habitable the attic space, is linked with the introduction of apsidal or elliptical plans having a straight facade; the long sides being barely curved, it was only the apse at the back that remained rounded and the plan as a whole was horseshoe-shaped. There is quite a long list of these buildings, which in the seventh and sixth centuries had a dual function, profane and religious. Within the great sanctuaries at Delphi and Delos, and on the Athenian acropolis, there were numerous chapels with an apsidal plan. The latest to be discovered and structurally the most interesting is that of Apollo Daphnephoros at Eretria. About thirty-eight feet long by twenty-five wide, the horseshoe plan has an entrance opening about six and one-half feet wide in the straight facade. Two pillars stood in front of this facade, almost in line with the side walls that supported a broad overhang of the roof, in the manner of the terra cotta model from the Argive Heraion. Inside, one post in line with the door and two others further back formed a triangle that served to support the roof framing; this consisted of a triangular truss at the facade end, and radial poles supporting the hip above the apse. The most original feature is in the two rows of bases, made of rammed clay and gravel; these bases are arranged in pairs on either side of the walls, and there are eleven groups of pairs, about ten feet apart. Thus the temple, inside and out, had a total of twenty-seven wood posts defining an unusual but very distinctive structure, of particular interest in relation to the history of the Greek house and temple at the beginning of the first millennium.

From these known elements in connection with the apsidal plan, there emerged the first examples of the columned porch intended to protect and enlarge the initial cell. In company with the Daphnephoreion of Eretria one should mention the megaron B of Apollo at Thermon, which is contemporary or a little later. Around the apsidal megaron, whose long sides are slightly curved, a series of slabs attests to the existence of a surrounding portico that supported either the overhang of the main roof or a lean-to. The posts were not continued across the front. The general lines were similar to those of the primitive temple at Eretria. These constitute the best examples of a still rudimentary architecture employing the "base" materials of wood, brick, rammed clay, rough stones—and perhaps even simple branches, as in the hut of laurel dedicated to Apollo, evoked by the texts in the Delphic

III. Athens, Temple of Athena Nike.

IV. Athens, south porch of the Erechtheion.

62. Delphi, Sanctuary of Apollo, trabeation from Treasury of the Siphnians. Delphi, Museum.

63. Athens, Acropolis, Olive-tree Pediment, of painted poros. Athens, Acropolis Museum.

sanctuary and illustrated by the finds at Eretria.

In the course of the sixth century Greek architecture succeeded in mastering the "noble" materials: limestone first, and then marble. Walls of rubble and brick were slowly transformed into a regular masonry of carefully hewn blocks—at that time called *plinthoi,* the same term used for bricks. The wood post became a trim stone column, at first fine and slender beneath an entablature that remained light; then that, too, was transformed from wood to stone.

During this process the architecture diversified its forms, specializing its shapes and plans as functions became ever more precisely defined. The city, itself more structured and organized, translated these trends into a varied and vigorous architecture whose subdivisions we must now examine in more detail.

RELIGIOUS ARCHITECTURE: MASTERPIECES OF THE IONIC ORDER

The most ancient remains of religious architecture, in which coexist the new forms and the older Aegean tradition, are found in two different parts of the Greek world.

First, in Crete, the primitive temples of Prinias and Dreros stand apart from the apsidal structures of mainland Greece. Their plans recall the Minoan chapels; squarish or oblong, the buildings incorporate sacrificial altars, libation tables, and benches for offerings and divine effigies. The enlarged interior required intermediate posts to support the terrace roof. The shape of the pillars, the predominance of uneven rhythms, and the taste for painted and sculptured borders around the openings and at the eaves reveal the bond between these archaic structures (eighth to seventh centuries) and the Minoan heritage.

Further east, on Delos and Samos in particular, these features, still recognizable in the Delian sanctuaries of Apollo and Artemis and of Leto, evolved rapidly into a broader, more monumental conception unmistakably influenced by the luxuriant Egyptian colonnade.

The requirements of ritual and worship had led to the creation of new forms adapted to a specific religious function. On the banks of the Imbrasos River, not far from the town of Samos, the effigy of Hera brought by the Argonauts was venerated beneath a baldachin among open-air altars and clumps of sacred willow. These were permanent elements of the cult that never disappeared, despite the multiple architectural transformations that the sanctuary underwent in the course of the centuries. The first Hecatompedon ("hundred-footer"; 100 by 20 feet) was built at the beginning of the eighth century; it was a large, very elongated hall whose roof was supported by an axial row of interior pillars. Soon there came to the fore the same preoccupation as at Thermon: by the end of the century the volume and monumentality were augmented by a peristyle of wood pillars, seven by

seventeen, the first manifestation of the peripteral plan.

During the first half of the seventh century, around 660 B.C., this building was replaced by a new temple, differently conceived and better adapted to the cult. A cella 101 feet long and over 21 feet wide, preceded by a tetrastyle vestibule, was surrounded by an eighteen-by-six-column peristyle (124 by 29 feet). The interior was largely unobstructed, the better to display the cult statue. The axial row of columns was eliminated and the weight of the roof was distributed among square pillars attached to the inside faces of the walls; these pillars stood on a light stylobate in exact correspondence with the columns of the exterior peristyle. These elements were now harmonized and coordinated, a notable advance in the composition of the building.

Further progress was made in the decade about 570-560 B.C. by the architects Rhoikos and Theodoros, who built the great Temple of Hera at Samos; and Theodoros, at least, in collaboration with Chersiphron the Cretan and his son Metagenes, also contributed to the building of the Artemision of Ephesus. These men belonged to that first generation of great Greek builders whose vigorous powers of creation and exceptional technical mastery enabled them to purge their art of groping primitivism. They were sculptors and engineers as well as architects, and filled with curiosity about the outside world—the two Samian architects traveled to Egypt—and, in the image of their times, they were preoccupied by technique and inclined toward ingenious research: "Theodoros," Pliny the Elder tells us, "who built the labyrinth of Samos [the great dipteral temple], made a statue of himself in bronze. This brought him fame not only because of the astonishing likeness of the portrait but also because of the great cunning of his art." Among themselves, moreover, they established the tradition of commentaries written by great artists on their works. The rare echoes of these writings that one finds in Vitruvius and Pliny make one regret the loss of a technical and theoretical literature that would have enlightened us on many aspects of Greek architectural creation.

The remains of the great Temple of Hera at Samos are all we have left from which to judge the work of Rhoikos and Theodoros. The scale is now vastly greater (347 by 173 feet); the peristyle is doubled to form a near "labyrinth" of 104 columns, their rhythm being established by the spacing of the interior columns of the temple; the intervals between the center facade columns, reflecting the interior columns and walls of the cella, were much greater (27 feet) than the side intervals (17 feet).

The Artemision at Ephesus, a contemporary work and equally huge (380 by 182 feet), surpassed its rival in richness of decoration. Likewise dipteral in plan, it had an octastyle facade (the rear facade had nine columns) and similar variations in the widths of the bays. The sculptural decoration, which the Classical epoch would confine to certain specific zones, here curiously spread over the outer columns of the facades: the lowest drum of each column, resting on an elaborately molded base with a double scotia surmounted by a torus, was decorated in low relief—unless, according to

a more recent hypothesis, the decoration was indeed located at the top, beneath the capital. Croesus, the wealthy king of Lydia, evidently intended to offer some of these sumptuous columns to the great goddess of Ephesus; several of them are inscribed with his name.

For hundreds of years the forms and motifs of Ionic architecture in Asia continued to be modeled on these two buildings; when the temples at Ephesus and at Sardis were rebuilt in the fourth century only the details were changed. The novel proportions, and new ideas of Hellenistic architects were necessary to bring fresh decoration to Magnesia on the Meander, and to Didyma.

From its domain in Asia Minor certain echoes of the Ionic style, at first timid and discreet, reached both inland Greece and the west, where the Doric order still reigned supreme. One receives the impression of a few variations grafted onto the basic theme.

In mainland Greece, the sanctuary of Apollo at Delphi and the Athenian acropolis have preserved the finest examples of Ionic architecture applied to buildings of modest proportions. These are refined, conceived as jewels, and intended to introduce into the sober Doric a bit of brightness and fantasy, to add decorative grace and charm to the more monumental displays in these sanctuaries. The treasuries of Delphi, the Temple of Athena Nike at the entrance to the Athenian acropolis, and the Erechtheion across from

67. *Athens, Acropolis, east portico, Temple of Athena Nike.*

68. *Athens, Acropolis, ceiling of portico, Temple of Athena Nike.*

the Parthenon relieve the relative severity of the great Doric structures.

In this miniature architecture the taste for sculptural decoration is most freely expressed in the Ionic treasuries of Delphi, dating from the period 550 to 525 B.C. In the treasuries of Clazomenae and of Marseilles the voluted capital of Asia Minor was replaced by a palm capital, doubtless based on an Egyptian model; the elongated leaves, their ends curled over, form a basket or *calathos.* The Cnidians, then the Siphnians, substituted for columns the figures of caryatids, closely related in style to the Archaic *korai.* The walls themselves bear molded and sculptured decorations: at the base is a strip of ornament, a grooved torus in the treasuries of Cnidos and Marseilles, a luxuriant bead-and-reel molding in that of Siphnos. At the top a sculptured frieze crowns the alternate courses of stretchers and headers. The architrave itself has a decoration of rosettes; it is separated from the frieze by a row of egg-and-dart ornaments. The frieze of warriors based on Homeric themes, beautifully carved in high relief of island marble, has touches of paint highlighting the sculptural effects. Finally, the soffit of the cornice that crowns the entablature is ornamented with a garland of palmettes and lotus flowers in a plump, expressive style.

Somewhat ostentatious efforts still accentuate the Ionian taste for decorative values, already perceptible in the great works of Rhoikos and Chersiphron. It ultimately modified the Asian scheme of the Ionic entablature by introducing a sculptured frieze to replace the dentils, those toothlike blocks projecting above the architrave in a decorative transforma-

69. *Athens, Acropolis, Erechtheion and Parthenon, from northwest.*

70. *Athens, Acropolis, north porch, Erechtheion, from northwest.*

tion of the beam-ends used in primitive construction to support the terrace roof. This was an insular feature of the Ionic order that only took hold in Asia Minor in the Hellenistic epoch.

On the Athenian acropolis, the Attic architects did not discount the decorative value of the Ionic style. They adopted it for small structures and introduced it into the interiors of Doric compositions, in both the Parthenon and the Propylaea. Callicrates, an architect in the service of Cimon who began to rebuild the acropolis between 460 and 451, designed the Temple of Athena Nike that projects like a figurehead at the entrance to the acropolis. A first version, built about 450, was the Temple of Demeter and Kore on the banks of the Ilissus River; it has since disappeared, but is known from the eighteenth-century accounts of Stuart and Revett. The Temple of Athena Nike was not built until about 420, at the end of the great Periclean phase. It is a successful Attic adaptation of island and Asian traditions. Almost square in plan—the cella is slightly wider than deep (13 feet 9 inches by 12 feet 5 inches)—it has the prostyle facade dear to the Athenians, the entrance portico in front of the vestibule. A columned order replaces the two columns in antis, a theme recalled at the corners of the rear wall; this has also a prostyle portico. The decorative value of the two facades—their deep-fluted monolithic columns resting on tall bases with grooved torus, and crowned with vigorous, amply voluted capitals—contrasts sharply with the deliberately bare walls of fine blocks of Pentelic marble, hewn and laid in accordance with the perfect regularity of the isodomic bond. At the same time, unity is established by the recurring grooved torus around the foot

71. *Athens, Acropolis, northeast corner of north porch, Erechtheion, showing lower portion of Ionic order.*

72. *Athens, Acropolis, northeast corner of north porch, Erechtheion, showing upper portion of Ionic order.*

of the wall, and by the sculptured frieze that surrounds the walls as well as the facades. The same movement associating architecture and decoration was continued in the panels of the balustrade along the edge of the bastion; reliefs of winged Victories evoked the various moments of the procession and sacrifices celebrated in honor of Athena Nike.

Toward the center of the acropolis, north of the Parthenon, rises the Erechtheion; the complexity of this temple, imposed by cult requirements and religious functions, finds resolution in the freedom and imaginativeness of the Ionic style. It is a veritable repertory of late fifth-century decorative forms assembled in a building that does not quite succeed in assimilating them all into a genuine architectural unity. The Erechtheion, begun about 421 and completed in the final years of the century, is the first work to introduce rococo into Classical harmony and simplicity.

The building consists of a rectangular core (38 by 75 feet) to which various elements are annexed. On the east, the facade is composed of a prostyle hexastyle Ionic portico of six columns. Opposite, on the west side, were four supports in a mixed order—Ionic half columns associated with half pilasters; a low balustrade originally ran between the supports, replaced in Roman times by a windowed wall. The west facade rests on a solid wall that forms a plinth to compensate for the ten-foot difference in grade between east and

75. *Athens, Acropolis, south porch, with caryatids, Erechtheion.*

76. *Xanthos, structural diagram of Monument of the Nereids (from Demargne-Coupel, 1969).*

77, 78. *Xanthos, isometric diagram of interior and reconstruction of Monument of the Nereids (from Demargne-Coupel, 1969).*

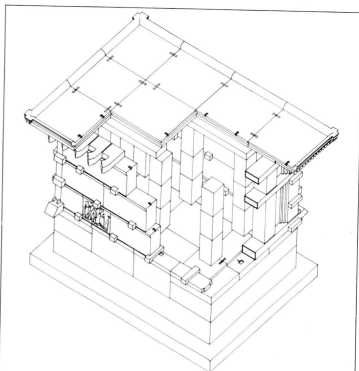

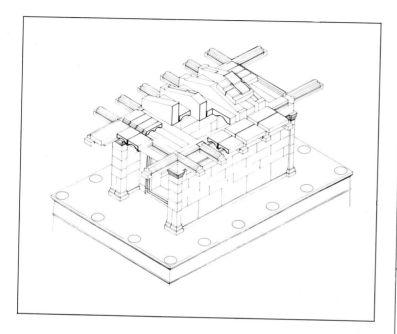

west. The interior is divided into four rooms, one open to the east, the others communicating with the north porch; these divide the space among the several deities to whom the shrine is dedicated.

The north portico, a gem of the Ionic style with four columns across the front and one behind at either side, extends straight out from the wall. Independently beautiful, it destroys the total unity. The columns combine lightness of proportion with vigorous flutings and graceful decoration: the upper torus of the Attic bases are decorated with interlaces; broad neckings are carved with anthemion ornament; the capitals have wide volutes whose spirals are underlaid by fillets. The portico shelters a monumental doorway whose jambs and lintels are richly framed with carved moldings and bands of egg-and-tongue and leaf-and-dart ornament. The opening is crowned by a cornice profiled with honeysuckle, where palmettes and lotus flowers nestle in the curve of the cyma; acanthus cups and elegant convolvulus spill from the spiral consoles at either side. The entablature frieze echoes the frieze on the outer walls and is treated in the same manner: figures carved in the round from white marble are set against slabs of blue Eleusinian marble.

On the south, another baldachin conceals the steps in the southwest corner of the building that gave access to the tomb of Cecrops, legendary king of Athens. This is the famous Caryatid portico. Sturdy maidens, the napes of their necks reinforced by wavy locks, support a dentiled Ionic

79. Xanthos, new restoration of
Monument of the Nereids. London,
British Museum.

entablature that contrasts with the ornamental frieze above it on the wall against which it rests.

Such, in broad outline, is the Erechtheion, in which are gathered all the innovations that the architects of fifth-century Athens tried to introduce into the decorative repertory of their art. Certain forms and details were later borrowed from the building, but it was too complicated, the cleavage between its architectural functions and decorative values too deep, to have ever served as a model. It remains a witness to the experiments at the end of the Classical epoch, a prelude to the great creative movement in the fourth century and Hellenistic period.

The Attic tendency to confine the use of the Ionic order to buildings of modest proportions set a fashion in the fourth century, particularly in funerary architecture. Two monuments of exceptional importance belong to this tradition, which persisted into Hellenistic and Roman times: the Nereid monument at Xanthos and the Mausoleum at Halicarnassus. They are alike both in their funerary character and in their structure, a curious blend of "barbarian" elements—Lycian and Anatolian—with Greek forms superficially applied.

The idea of a monument raised upon a terrace, and comprising a tall massive podium supporting an Ionic chapel—further developed at Halicarnassus by a huge stepped pyramidal base that supports a crowning marble quadriga with statues of Mausolos and his wife—had already become a reality in Lycian heroic monuments of the sixth and fifth centuries. These stone copies of primitive wooden structures, in technique purely Lycian and Anatolian, had nothing in common with Greek architecture. The use of figured friezes at the top of terrace walls, or to crown a plinth, is more Oriental than Greek. The transformation of these indigenous monuments was a consequence of the penetration of Greek influence and of the Hellenizing policies practiced by the native princes or Persian satraps; local and traditional structures were simply clothed in Greek forms.

The terrace, supported by a handsome, regularly bonded stone wall, was ornamented with sculptured figures (Nereids on the acropolis of Xanthos, lions on Halicarnassus); the podium was itself decorated with one or two friezes whose subjects were sometimes drawn from Greek mythology but often borrowed from the triumphal themes of the Oriental repertory (processions of chariots, combat, the hunt, etc.); finally, the chapel forsook the geometric forms of Oriental tradition and assumed the guise of a small Greek temple: an Ionic building either in antis or peripteral; Ionic columns with bases and capitals in the Asian style; entablature with sculptured decoration, doors embellished with egg-and-tongue ornament, volutes, and palmettes. The very fame of these monuments and their success as funerary architecture bear witness to the remarkable decorative value of the Ionic style as developed by the first Ionian architects of the sixth century, modified and perfected by fifth-century Athenians. This was the heritage that artists of the Hellenistic epoch were to exploit.

80. *Thermon, painted terra cotta metope from Temple of Apollo. Athens, National Museum.*

81. *Halicarnassus, amazon frieze from Mausoleum, by Scopas. London, British Museum.*

THE DORIC ORDER: INFANCY AND YOUTH

In the second half of the seventh century B.C. religious architecture, in mainland Greece and the west, found in the Doric style the forms and features that enabled the Doric order, within a few decades, to achieve its most balanced expression.

The Peloponnesus was the birthplace of the Doric column with its fluted shaft, planted directly on the stylobate with no base or transitional molding, and its flattened capital, whose broadly projecting echinus is separated from the shaft by vigorous annulets with a sculptured necking of curling leaves fringing a necking groove of variable depth. The square abacus above is never omitted. Was the Doric an adaptation of the Mycenaean capital, which also had a necking groove and a very thick torus? or an independent Dorian invention?

The evidence suggests that the form may have been derived from an ancient prototype, versions of which are to be found forming part of the facade of the "Treasury of Atreus" and the relief of the Lion Gate at Mycenae. It is hardly surprising therefore that the earliest Doric capitals come from Tiryns, Mycenae, and Argos, or from the older Dorian colonies at Syracuse, Megara Hyblaea, and Selinus. Was this the order of the first peristyle temple, erected on the highest terrace of the Heraion of Argos in the mid-seventh century? In any event, the broad lines of the order were established in the temples of Apollo, Artemis, and Hera, at Thermon (c. 620–610), Corfu (c. 600), and Olympia (c. 600) respectively, even before the transformation from wood to stone was completed. The columns were still of wood; they sometimes rested on stone plinths that protected the foot of the post; they were crowned by stone capitals. Architraves of wood and friezes of brick and terra cotta added to this strange mixture, whose polychromy was particularly lively. The metopes and cymas at Thermon, of terra cotta in the Geometric Corinthian style, attest to the importance of the northeast Peloponnesus in creating and developing the Doric order. The plan is elongated (5 by 15 columns at Thermon, 8 by 17 at Corfu); the cella already has interior supports (two rows of columns at Corfu) or spur walls and intermediate columns in the Heraion at Olympia (where the peristyle of 6 by 16 columns is more regular); there is always a pronaos, less systematically a rear vestibule or opisthodomos. The rhythms of the Olympian Heraion, with its division into five small chapels on each side wall, are complex; they betray the perplexity of the architects, confronted with the extended scale demanded by the triumphal monumentality of the period, and by the transition from simple linear construction to the new subtlety of internal volumes and external masses. The porticoes reflect this process in their greater thickness and heaviness of proportion, which at first had retained the lightness and slimness of wood construction. More than a century was needed to recover the slenderness of the *poros* limestone column of the first Temple of Athena at Delphi (c. 600 B.C.).

The technique seems to hesitate in substituting one material for another.
There was still uncertainty about the strength of stone when used in these
varied places: proportions were strengthened, spans diminished, and points
of stress were modified. A fine example of this cautious experimentation
is provided by the Treasury in the sanctuary of Hera at the mouth of the
Sele River, five miles north of Paestum. Though constructed as late as 560
to 540 B.C., it clearly illustrates the ingenuity of the Archaic builders, still
relatively unfamiliar with the qualities of the new material. The Treasury
was a rectangular building, without a peristyle. The east porch had two
columns with Doric capitals firmly profiled and vigorously set off by fillets
carved at the base of the echinus; these contrast with the delicacy of the anta
capitals decorated with palmettes and lotus flowers which are not integrated
with, but applied to, the ends of the walls. The antae are not load-bearing;
they are merely decorative, like the primitive boards that held up, in brick
construction, the somewhat fluctuating projection of walls.

The builder was equally mistrustful of the entablature, despite the vigor
of its frieze of sculptured metopes framed by emphatic triglyphs, carved
separately and projecting strongly. It is, in fact, merely a screen erected in
front of the timber framing that supported the roof; this structure has left
marks on the inside faces of the frieze blocks. The sculptured metopes of
the frieze were slid in between the triglyphs, and notches in the back face
show that they were installed when the timber framing was already in place.
This framing was composed of vertical and horizontal members pegged
together to form a rigid structure capable of carrying the horizontal ceiling
beams; these beams rested in between, on three interior supports—one, as
in the Daphnephoreion of Eretria, nearer to the doubtless pedimented
facade and the other two paired at the back to carry the radial hip rafters.
The main rafters were stiffened by posts that rested on the horizontal beams.
Altogether a remarkable survival of Archaic building methods in a part of
the Greek world already well acquainted with a variety of extremely
vigorous, though still immature, works in the Doric style. Powerful and
severe, its lines sober yet capable of flowering into massive, well-balanced
compositions, this style expressed the raw energy of the young Greek
colonies in the west. They had been formed in a hard school but they quickly
prospered and were eager to express their new character and magnificence.
The grand buildings at Syracuse, Selinus, Acragas, and Paestum were the
outcome of this fortunate conjunction of ample material resources and a
politico-religious spirit anxious to assert itself through an architecture of
extraordinary promise.

The earliest and crudest of these temples was the Apolloneion built about
570–560 B.C. on Ortygia, the island just off Syracuse. Already regular in
plan, peripteral and hexastyle (6 by 17 columns) and measuring 71 feet wide
and 183 feet long, it simultaneously expresses both the clumsiness and the
pride of the architects and stone carvers, Kleomenes and Epikles, who
incised their names on one step of the crepidoma cut in enormous monolithic

83. Olympia, Terrace of the Treasuries and entrance to stadium, from west.

84. Olympia, view toward palaestra, from south.

85. Paestum, Sele River, reconstruction of facade of Treasury, Sanctuary of Hera (from Zancani-Montuoro and Zanotti-Blanco, 1951).

86. Paestum, Sele River, plan of Treasury, Sanctuary of Hera (from Zancani-Montuoro and Zanotti-Blanco, 1951).

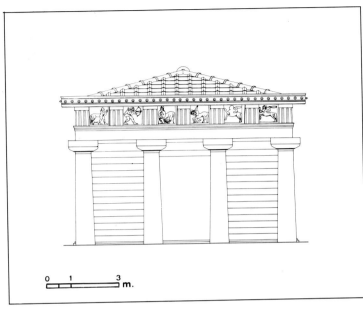

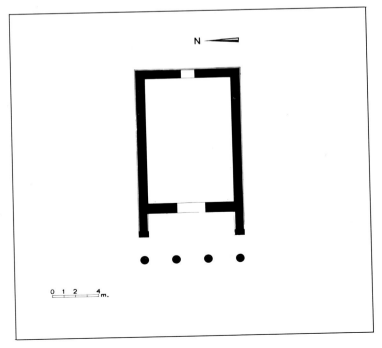

V. Olympia, Temple of Hera.

87, 88. *Paestum, Sele River, two metopes from Treasury, Sanctuary of Hera.*

89. *Paestum, Sele River, reconstructed frieze of Treasury, Sanctuary of Hera. Paestum, Museum.*

90. *Paestum, Sele River, transverse section of Treasury, Sanctuary of Hera (from Zancani-Montuoro and Zanotti-Blanco, 1951).*

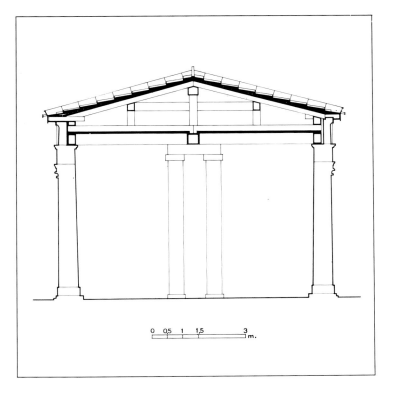

blocks. The columns are cramped and heavy (diameter 6 feet 7 inches; interaxial dimension 13 feet 7 inches; height 26 feet 2 inches); the entablature is crushing (nearly 22 feet high), worthy of the impressive consumption of materials represented by this early example of Syracusan architecture, which was never to lose its taste for strength and power.

The architects of Magna Graecia very rapidly mastered the materials and principles of the Doric order. In the middle of the sixth century (550–540) Temple C, the first of the great temples at Selinus, was erected within the already ancient sanctuary that occupied the southeast portion of the acropolis. Everything here is light and airy, an expression of the creative freedom of the Sicilian architects. The elongated plan is in the tradition of the early cult megarons of Selinus; the long narrow cella, with an adyton (sacristy) at the back, appears to stand independently inside the colonnade (6 by 15 columns), from which it is separated by a wide gallery (nearly 21 feet); in front, a double row of columns accentuated the disengagement of the principal spaces, the handsome mass being thrown into relief by a flight of eight steps stretching the full width of the facade. The rhythm of the colonnade is perfectly free, not governed by the internal divisions of the cella; the interaxial dimension of the facade columns is 14 feet 6 inches; those on the sides are closer (12 feet 9 inches), and the diameters fluctuate between 60 and 72 inches. Here the Doric style is animated by a precise sense of plasticity and a refined exploitation of the contrast between light and shade. The entablature, thanks to the energy of its forms, is full of movement. The frieze and the cornice are very strongly modeled, the triglyphs projecting forward from the plane of the metopes, and the mutules and guttae having imposing volume. The same concern also accentuates the ten sculptured metopes. The subjects, detached from the background by their high relief, were framed by flat slabs that made the figures stand out as if on a stage: Apollo driving a quadriga, seen in front view; Perseus beheading Medusa; Heracles striding along with two Cercopes slung over his shoulders. Finally, the edge of the roof had a splendid revetment of painted terra cottas, the facing of the beams that crowned the entablature as well as the cyma proper, all ornamented with clear-cut palmette and lotus motifs.

This was the first big project of the Sicilian workshops, which for more than a century continued to produce these original works that were used throughout southern Italy: Selinus, Syracuse, Gela, Locri, Metapontum, and Paestum all showed rich ensembles of architectural terra cottas. These have such pictorial and monumental value that some were exported to Greece itself; the Treasury of Gela at Olympia is a good example of this.

The architects of Western Greece, i.e., Sicily and South Italy, throughout the sixth century and the first half of the fifth remained faithful to the Doric style, with such exceptions as Syracuse and Locri. They employed it flexibly, however, with more liberty than the builders of mainland Greece, who were quickly trapped in the rigid rules of the order; the western architects had

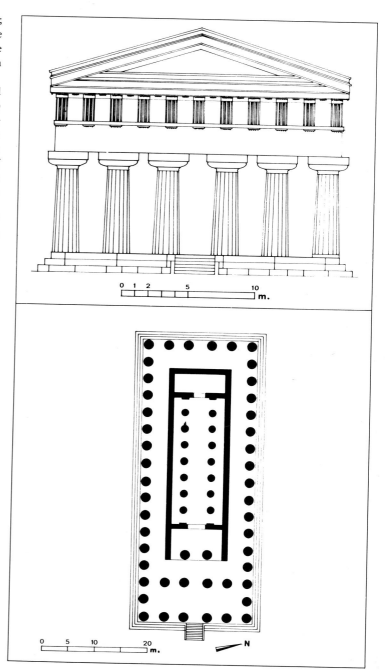

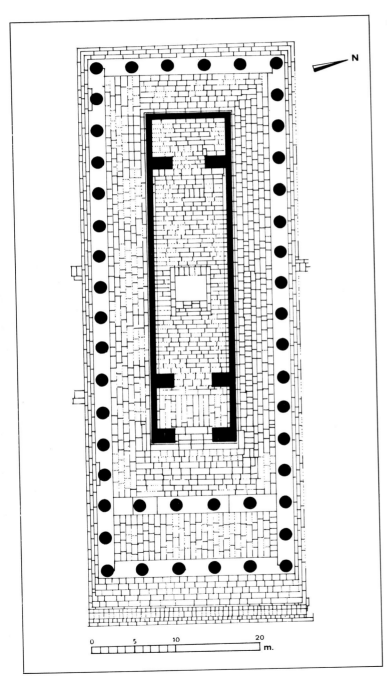

94. *Selinus, plan of Temple C (from Bervé-Gruben, 1962).*

N

0   5   10   20
m.

a more developed taste for the monumental, a keener appreciation of the relations between masses and volumes, and a refined sense of architectural plasticity.

In proof of these statements, a few examples may be cited. First, there is the tendency to proceed by juxtaposition, by playing off one building against another; this concerns architectural composition and the organization of space, questions to which we shall return later on. The acropolis of Selinus with its four great temples; the sacred hill of Marinella nearby with all the variants represented by its three temples, E, F, and G; the string of temples that fringed the southern edge of the city of Acragas; the sacred area of Paestum whose temenos wall borders the great north-south axis; the massive remains of the temples erected within the temenos of the Lycian Apollo in the very heart of the city of Metapontum—all of these reflect a systematically developed concept of monumentality doubtless linked with the expression of material power and the manifestation of an effective political ascendancy, but also with the more or less conscious desire to ensure the good will and protection of the traditional gods for these colonial cities in a land that was not always favorable or even friendly.

The details of each building reveal the spirit of independence and the originality of western Doric by numerous innovations. Since there can be no question of studying each temple individually, a few pertinent examples will suffice to illustrate this point. At Selinus, on the hill of Marinella, each temple had its own distinct physiognomy; the imposing mass of Temple G was offset by the lighter, more graceful, and yet more mysterious silhouette of Temple F, of which the pteron was sealed off, doubtless for some ritual purpose, by a wall extending halfway up the slender columns. Temple E, to the south, with its poised, more classical lines, is the only one so far restored and thus sets the scale for this grandiose landscape.

Temple G, dedicated to Apollo or Zeus, was one of the finest and most ambitious realizations of the Doric order in Western Greece. Temple F still retains the Archaic features of temples C and D on the Selinus acropolis in its elongated proportions (132 by 30 feet) and tripartite cella, and the spirit of Temple C is further reflected in the treatment of the intercolumnial voids (intervals of 14 feet 9 inches in the facade and 15 feet 2 inches along the sides, with a diameter of 5 feet 11 inches at the foot of the columns) and in the lightness of the colonnade. The Apolloneion, Temple G, has another object in view. The tyrant Peithagoras, who presided over the groundbreaking ceremonies about 520 and doubtless commissioned the enterprise, was certainly bent on rivaling the great temples of Ionia, but the architect succeeded in adapting to this project the possibilities of the Doric order.

The proportions of Temple G (363 by 165 feet) are those of the colossal sanctuaries of Ephesus and Samos, but volume and space are handled in a totally different spirit. Accumulations of columns, sometimes loaded with sculpture, have given place to broad spaces; the external colonnade (8 by

17 columns) is not doubled as in the dipteral plan, but the pteron itself is wide enough to include a double row (almost 40 feet), and is a nave in itself. The cella departed from the traditional Sicilian plan: the adyton, it is true, was preserved, but transformed into an independent chapel at the end of the cella; this was a vast hall 60 feet wide, divided into three equal aisles by a double row of columns; it was, no doubt, only partially roofed over, but it was intended to be entirely enclosed and the temple was not meant to be hypaethral. Possibly during construction some influence was exerted by the example of the Didymaion and its interior chapel. The treatment of the cella entrance is also conservative: a prostyle porch consisting of four columns in advance of two aligned with the ends of the walls, it is no longer independent of the peristyle; the supports, columns as well as antae, are all aligned with exterior columns. Thus, the plan as a whole is perfectly unified and all the traditional elements are interpreted harmoniously and flexibly in terms of space and volumes. This temple, in our opinion, is the finest achievement of Doric architecture in Sicily and Magna Graecia.

At about the same time an attempt was made at Syracuse to introduce the Ionic order. About 525 B.C., in the sanctuary where the Temple of Athena was to be built at the beginning of the fifth century, the close relations between Sicily and Ionia, discernible in commerce and the other arts, resulted in the choice of the Aegean Ionic style for this temple, whose dimensions were the same as those of the later Athenaion (about 195 by 83 feet), but the plan and the proportions remained Doric. The style of the column bases and capitals was influenced by the architecture of the coast of Asia Minor. Though it remained an isolated attempt, it is evidence of a penetration of which traces are to be found at Megara Hyblaea, at Gela, even at Selinus, and still more distinctly in the Achaean colonies of Magna Graecia, where the Doric tradition was less deeply rooted.

The architecture at Paestum is quite typical of the suppleness introduced by the Ionian trend into the details of an order that had never become fixed in solid structures.

The older (c. 530 B.C.) of the two temples of Hera at Paestum, that known as the Basilica, has a number of noteworthy features. To begin with the plan, there is an odd number of columns in the facade (9 by 18 columns; 81 by 179 feet). The disruptive effects of this are also apparent in the interior of the building: the cella is divided into two equal aisles by one axial colonnade; the pronaos has two doors into the nave, one for each aisle, and in front three columns in antis. The architect has struggled to bind the elements of the plan together: the long pterons correspond in width to exactly two intercolumniations, and the cella walls and the three columns of the vestibule are aligned with the five central columns of both east and west facades. The cross walls correspond with peristyle columns, so that the entire area enclosed by the peristyle is geometrically divided into four equal parts, though for practical reasons the principle could not be applied to the building in detail. In order to free sufficient space at the end of the cella

for the cult statue, the interior columns were spaced wider toward the west; consequently, they are unrelated with the peristyle columns. The Ionian taste of the decoration is displayed in the treatment of the capitals, foliated grooves underscoring the heavily flattened echinus, and in the details of the entablature, where the flat band of the architrave has been replaced by a cyma with Lesbian leaves.

A similar molding enriched with egg-and-tongue ornament was doubtless introduced in the nearby Temple of Athena and in the great Heraion on the Sele River, both built around 500 B.C. These two temples went even further in seeking plastic effects, multiplying the decorative courses and transforming the mutuled taenia. In the sanctuary on the Sele the taenia was replaced by an only slightly projecting molded course, which accentuated the height of the entablature; the raking cornice of the Temple of Athena projected far enough to have coffers beneath, decorated with gilded bronze rosettes. Here, the Ionic order has crept even into the interior of the Doric shell. The architect has preserved the monumental character of the cella; as in certain temples at Selinus, it has a prostyle portico (4 by 2 columns) with half columns at the ends of the walls, but the order is Ionic and the capital belongs to a series familiar in Asia Minor and different from the Samian Ionic types; the proportions are less elongated, the central mass is plumper, the ample volutes are compressed against the shaft.

None of these innovations is to be found in the last temple at Paestum, the Temple of Hera II (Poseidon) erected in the middle of the fifth century near the Basilica. Here, all the rules of the Classical Doric order are respected: regular plan of cella with pronaos and opisthodomos; principal chamber divided into three aisles by two Doric colonnades, each with a superimposed order; design and proportions of the entablature comparable to the temples of mainland Greece, such as those of Zeus at Olympia and of Athena Aphaia on Aegina.

Thus at the beginning of the fifth century the rules of the Doric order

were imposed in both Magna Graecia and Sicily, but their application preserves a freedom and flexibility from the Archaic heritage and from innovative traditions proper to Western Greece. This originality will become confirmed as we pursue our study of Doric religious architecture on mainland Greece and in the west.

DORIC RELIGIOUS ARCHITECTURE: MATURITY

On mainland Greece, the birthplace of the Doric order, the early Doric monuments lack the flavor of those in the west; the age of masterpieces begins only with the period around 500 B.C.

Of course, there are numerous and varied buildings whose Archaic features and other particularities permit us to follow the progress of the order. One of the oldest and most significant is the Temple of Artemis on Corfu; erected at the beginning of the sixth century during Corfu's flourishing years as a staging point for colonists on their way to Italy and Sicily, the temple reveals the innate potential of the Doric style. The long cella (116 by 31 feet) with pronaos and opisthodomos, divided into three aisles by two rows of ten columns, is surrounded by an impressive peristyle of 8 by 17 columns (depth of pteron 21 feet 6 inches), whose capitals are among the best balanced of the Archaic series. The proportions of the order are robust but not at all massive; the entablature is also lightened by the mixture of materials, stone and terra cotta, and animated by the lively polychromy that accents the geometric and plant motifs of the decoration; the pediment already begins its sculptural role with the imposing Gorgon who assures the protection of the edifice.

At this point, a more technical and more detailed account would have to introduce the aediculae and treasuries of the great sanctuaries, in particular Delphi's ancient tholos and the Sicyonian peristyle decorated with a series of metopes of thoroughly Peloponnesian inspiration. Numerous fragments of the *poros* treasuries preserve curious formal peculiarities which

100. Selinus (Marinella), cella of Temple E (Hera), from east.

101. Selinus (Marinella), metope of Artemis and Actaeon, from Temple E (Hera). Palermo, Archaeological Museum.

102. *Acragas, air view of Temple of Juno Lacinia (Temple D).*

103. *Acragas, interior of Temple of Juno Lacinia (Temple D), from southeast.*

mark the progressive elaboration of the Classical style. Corinth certainly played an important part in the development of this architecture and still, in addition to numerous ruins, retains the mighty Temple of Apollo, not to mention that of Poseidon in its sanctuary at the Isthmus. A few heavy columns of the Apolloneion, which dominated the agora at Corinth, still stand out against the somber background of Acrocorinth. It influenced the builders of the Old Temple of Athena on the Athenian acropolis and of the Temple of Apollo at Delphi, which replaced and eclipsed the structure dating from the beginning of the century. The peristyle of the unfinished Old Temple of Athena was modeled on that of the temple at Corinth, with its slightly squatter columns, irregular rhythm of the bays (13 feet 4 inches in the front facade, 12 feet 8 inches along the sides), and shortened corner interaxials; even the cella had the same two-chamber plan.

Nor did the two sons of Pisistratus show much originality when they started in the mid-sixth century to build the Temple of Zeus, south of the Athenian acropolis on the banks of the Ilissus; drawing inspiration from the works of the tyrant Polycrates of Samos, they adopted a dipteral Ionian plan of ample proportions (356 by 135 feet; 108 columns distributed in two rows down the long sides and three rows of eight columns at front and rear). The plan scarcely reflects the usual style of the tyrants' architects, of whom Vitruvius mentions four: Antistates, Callaischros, Antimachides, and Porinos. The irregularity of the bays in the facade, copied from Ephesian and Samian temples, is not compatible with the strict requirements imposed by a Doric frieze, with its regular alternation of triglyphs and metopes; moreover, the heaviness of the columns (diameter at the base almost eight feet) and the shortening of the side spans contrast oddly with a light Ionic entablature. Work was interrupted by the fall of the tyrants in 510 B.C., not to be resumed for three centuries.

In truth, it was only with the early fifth-century temples at Aegina and Olympia, and finally with the Parthenon, that the Doric order came into its own, before undergoing the transformations in the following century that led to its decline.

The Temple of Aphaia on the eastern tip of the island of Aegina combines the energy and life of Archaism with the elegance and poise of the Classical style. Quite small in size (95 by 45 feet) and hexastyle in plan (6 by 12 columns), it is built of local limestone that blends in perfectly with the surrounding landscape, from which it seems to draw the harmony and exquisite balance of its forms and volumes. The columns, many still coated with the pale stucco that concealed the pores and irregularities of the bluish-gray stone, are light and slender; the ratio of the diameter at the base of the column to its height is in this case 1:5.32, whereas at Corinth it was 1:4.15. The delicate, almost immaterial lines of the flutings lead the eye upward to the supple profile of the capital, in which the strength of the Archaic echinus has not yet been displaced by the purely functional stiffness of its Classical counterpart. There is here no compromise with foreign influences nor distortion of Doric geometry in the interests of any decorative concern; the cool, pure play of simple lines and harmonious volumes constitutes the charm of this architecture, so perfectly at home in the island landscape.

The cella is thoroughly Classical, with pronaos and opisthodomos, each opening on a portico with two columns in antis. Despite its narrowness (21 feet) it is divided into three aisles by two double-storied Doric colonnades; the role of these is more decorative than structural, and a fifth-century architect would have had no compunction about bridging so modest a span without the upper colonnades. But they formed the setting, required by the Classical plan, within which were displayed the cult statue and its baldachin, elements associated with the play of columns—not without difficulty in a center aisle only ten feet wide.

Slightly later another building, the Treasury of the Athenians at Delphi, achieved the same high level in the harmony of its Doric forms. Its youthful vigor and flexibility are characteristic of the brief moment of balance between the sometimes overpowering weight of Archaic structures and the cold severity of the Classical style. Architecture and plastic art flow effortlessly together.

The Temple of Zeus at Olympia, perhaps because of the personality of its Peloponnesian architect, Libon, was built along heavier lines than the Temple of Aphaia at Aegina, though the latter is older; the principal edifice of the sanctuary of the Olympian Zeus certainly dates from the period 470–460 B.C. The extreme coarseness of the building material, shell limestone, was overcome by a coating of white marble stucco enlivened by vigorous polychromy; the blues and reds of the triglyphs contrasted with the milky whiteness of columns and walls. The sculptures in the east pediment glorified Zeus, the lord of these precincts, shown presiding over the chariot race in which Oenomaus died and Pelops triumphed; in the western pediment Apollo extends a protective arm over the Lapiths in their bitter combat with the Centaurs. In the half-light of the interior porticoes, high on the pronaos and opisthodomos walls, were twelve metopes portraying the labors of Heracles, in homage to the victories of the benevolent hero.

The massive temple rose above an artificial embankment that gave it a dominant position in the sacred wood. Its construction marked the beginning of an increasingly rigid application of the modular system which later architects would make into a rule that became often sterile. The rhythm of the colonnade was based on the standard interaxial dimension of sixteen Doric feet, and multiples or submultiples of this module are repeated in the cella (3 by 9 modules, or 48 by 144 feet) and in various parts of the entablature: one triglyph and metope together equal one-half module (8 feet); in the cornice, one mutule and via make one-quarter module (4 feet); while the tiles are one-eighth module (2 feet) wide.

In the three-aisled cella the gold-and-ivory statue of Zeus sat enthroned,

106. *Paestum, plan of Temple of
Hera I (Basilica) (from Bervé-
Gruben, 1962).*

107. *Paestum, Temple of Hera I
(Basilica) and Temple of Hera II
(Poseidon), from northeast.*

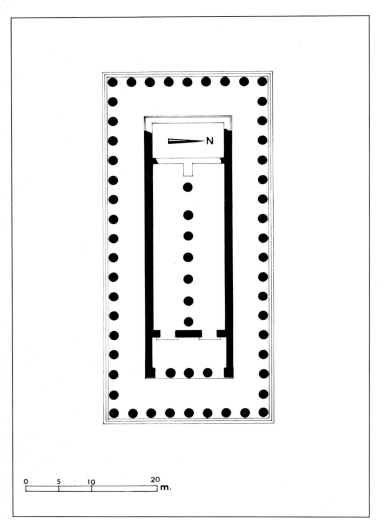

a masterpiece by Phidias; the sculptor's workshop has recently been
excavated and described, and the unusual finds include many of the artist's
tools and other traces of his activities. The double two-story Doric
colonnade, as usual dividing the cella into three parts, formed the setting
for the cult statue; its severity was moderated by the coloring of the floor,
composed of a mosaic of white pebbles, and by the decorative accessories
grouped around the statue that Pausanias listed in the second century A.D.
To judge from the literary testimony, Phidias' work was far from
harmoniously adapted to the architectural setting; the seated figure of Zeus
was too large to fit comfortably between the rows of columns. The architects
of the next generation were to have the task of creating, within the
traditional plan, a free and uncramped space capable of accommodating cult
groups whose scale and grandeur continually increased.

The true character of this architecture cannot be fully appreciated without
an effort to visualize the decoration. Moreover, one should never forget
the close ties that existed between architects and sculptors, and especially
between Ictinus and Phidias, the creators of the Parthenon. That great
temple of Athena Parthenos, the gem of Pericles' program for the Athenian
acropolis, occupies a privileged place in the history of Doric architecture.
Tied to the past by the need to conform to previous programs, it heralded
the profound transformations that were to mark the end of the predominance of the traditional Doric style and its gradual ousting by the Ionic and
Corinthian.

In 447 B.C., when work on the Parthenon entered a particularly active
phase, the site was far from being unencumbered and numerous constraints
imposed their limitations on the new architect. Without wanting to enter
into matters that are still under discussion, let us try and visualize the
approximate condition of the site handed over to Phidias and Ictinus.

The desolation that must have followed the agony of the Persian wars
and the occupation of the sacred rock by the Persians is chillingly conveyed
by Thucydides' restrained account. "As for the Athenians..., they began to
bring back their wives and children and what property they had left from
the places where they had hidden them away. They also started to rebuild
their city and their fortifications. For of their walls, little was left standing,
and as for their houses, most were in ruins; only the few that had been
occupied by high officers of the Persian army remained intact" (I, 89, 3).
Themistocles, faithful to his politics of grandeur, at first left aside the city
and its monuments to concentrate on rebuilding the city walls and equipping
the port of Piraeus, which was necessary to the economic independence of
Athens and the success of its expansionist foreign policy. The fortification
walls of the acropolis still confirm visually Thucydides' words, as he
continues: "It was thus that the Athenians fortified their city in a very short
time. Even today it is apparent that the building was done in haste. Indeed,
the lower courses consist of different sorts of stones, in some cases not shaped
to fit, but laid just as they were brought up at the time. Columns taken from

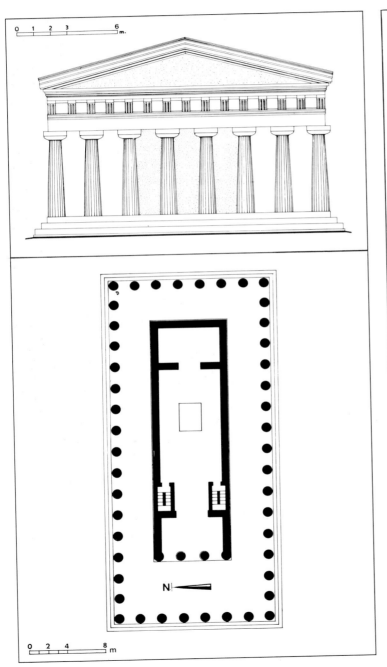

111. *Paestum, Sele River, elevation of Temple of Hera, Sanctuary of Hera (from Bervé-Gruben, 1962).*

112. *Paestum, Sele River, plan of Temple of Hera, Sanctuary of Hera (from Zancani-Montuoro and Zanotti-Blanco, 1951).*

113. *Paestum, Sele River, reconstruction of trabeation of Temple of Hera, Sanctuary of Hera (from Zancani-Montuoro and Zanotti-Blanco, 1951).*

114. *Paestum, Ionic capital from Temple of Athena. Paestum, Museum.*

115. *Locri, capital from Ionic temple. Reggio Calabria, National Museum.*

116. *Paestum, plan of Temple of Hera II (Poseidon) (from Bervé-Gruben, 1962).*

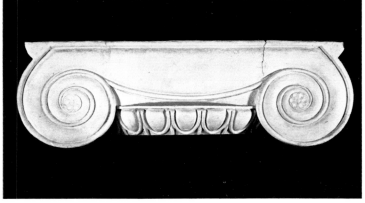

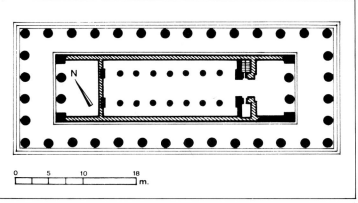

117. Paestum, Temple of Hera II (Poseidon), from northeast.

118, 119. Paestum, interior of Temple of Hera II (Poseidon), from west.

120. *Delphi, Sanctuary of Apollo. Reconstruction of ancient Tholos (from Charbonneaux-Martin-Villard, 1968).*

121. *Delphi, Sanctuary of Apollo, capitals of Sicyonian Treasury (on foundations).*

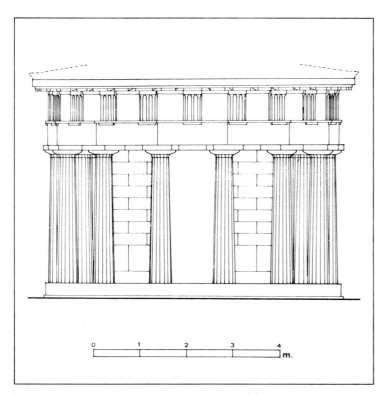

tombs and fragments of sculpture were mixed in freely with the rest."

The rebuilt ramparts of the acropolis consumed the columns and pieces of entablature intended for the first Parthenon. Only after the fortifications had been rebuilt and the city had erased the traces of invasion did the Athenians think anew of the gods and the acropolis. Cimon, with his well-known religious scruples, initiated the programs. It was first necessary to prepare the site and replace the ancient ramparts on the south. A vast filling and leveling operation made possible a southward extension of the platform on which the new temple was to be erected. A handsome wall, still well preserved, served both to protect the sanctuary and to retain the new terraces. This part of the program, accurately dated from the objects found among the fill, was certainly the work of Cimon. However it is not so certain, as recently suggested, that it was he and his architect, Callicrates, who resumed construction of the temple and carried it, on its south side at least, as far up as the entablature. There are both technical and chronological reasons for hesitating to follow the author of this suggestion in all his conclusions: it is hard to see how, after the death of Cimon and the disgrace of Callicrates, the entire southern colonnade could have been dismantled and rearranged to conform with the new plan of Phidias and Ictinus.

Cimon's share in the construction of the temple itself cannot be determined with precision; but however far the work had advanced, Phidias and Ictinus took over a site already containing construction. They were charged with the execution of a state commission, conceived and interpreted at Pericles' instigation as a design at once national and Panhellenic. A massive foundation originally laid of Piraeus limestone had by now become partly buried beneath Cimon's terracing. The crepidoma and certain elements of the colonnade, if not entire sections of the colonnade and entablature (as Rhys Carpenter maintains), were already in place. These imposed constraints from which there was no escape except by razing everything; this was impossible, because the siting of the structure was predetermined by the existing foundations and the nature of the terrain; the most that could be done was to lengthen it a little on the west and widen it on the north.

Actually the temple already begun corresponded to traditional structures at Aegina and Olympia. The plan was hexastyle (6 by 16 columns), the proportions elongated (221 by 78 feet); and, like the Temple of Apollo at Corinth and the Old Temple of Athena, its neighbor to the north, it had a two-chambered cella. The main hall was divided quite conventionally into three aisles by a double two-story row of ten columns; the second hall, more square in plan, had four columns, a formula repeated in the rear hall, or Parthenon, of the later Periclean structure. This traditional plan, however, failed to provide the space that Phidias needed for his gold-and-ivory statue; moreover, it was probably unsatisfactory to Pericles, who wished to make the new temple a symbol of Athenian greatness, perhaps even a reflection

122. *Corinth, Temple of Apollo, from northeast.*

123. *Corinth, Temple of Apollo, from north.*

IX. *Paestum, Temple of Hera I*
(Basilica).

X. *Paestum, Temple of Hera III*
(Poseidon).

125. Aegina, Temple of Aphaia,
from southwest.

of his Panhellenic ambitions. A more imposing external volume called for
a more vast and empty interior space.

No doubt for reasons of economy, the architect also found himself
compelled to use the Pentelic marble drums already hewn and placed in
position on the site; from the outset he was saddled with proportional
consequences imposed by the diameter of the columns.

The Parthenon was thus the result of a series of compromises between
sometimes contradictory requirements; in this way it becomes easier to
understand the anomalies and innovations, some of which were to have
far-reaching repercussions. The architect could not increase the interaxial
spans without upsetting the proportions established by the given diameter
of the columns; in order to enlarge the interior he introduced additional
columns in the peristyle, adopting the unorthodox rhythm of eight columns
in the facade instead of six, and seventeen along the sides instead of sixteen.
The width of the pteron was reduced, which made it possible to widen the
cella to 62 feet 6 inches; the resulting building was only slightly longer than
before (229 feet, instead of 221), but considerably wider (102 feet, instead
of 78 feet). To support the enlarged superstructure the foundations were
extended to the north, onto the rocky plateau where no terracing was
needed. The pronaos and opisthodomos were reduced to the minimum,
their facades accentuated by a second row of columns in conformity with
the prostyle arrangement adopted in the original plan.

These changes, as archaeological observations have confirmed, were so
cleverly calculated as to enable the architect to establish within the new
structures a close modular relationship that was based on the very dimension
he had been forced to accept—namely, the diameter of the base of the
columns. The ratio of this diameter (75 inches) to the typical interaxial
dimension (170 inches) is 4:9. The same ratio is repeated in the dimensions
of the stylobate (length 228 feet, width 102 feet), and in the corresponding
dimensions of the cella; it also appears in the elevations: the width of the
facade to its height (up to the horizontal cornice beneath the pediment).
These proportions are inscribed within the pyramiding movement involving
all the external lines: the curvature of the stylobate is reflected in the
entablature; the columns incline inward and toward the diagonals. The
architect found in this system of simple ratios and geometric relations a sort
of guaranty against effects of dispersion that might have resulted from so
difficult and complex a project.

Having established the exterior contours and volumes, Ictinus was free
to provide the liberal interior spaces required by the sculptor. He retained
the two halls from the previous structure. The smaller, opening to the west
beneath the opisthodomos, had the same square arrangement of four
columns springing straight to the roof. Ictinus chose the Ionic style as more
appropriate to such tall proportions, a notable decision that introduced the
Ionic order into an otherwise wholly Doric building. This innovation
opened the way to a mixing of styles in an architecture previously much

91

concerned about homogeneity; thenceforth the advance of the Ionic style was not to be restrained.

In the great hall, the convention of a two-story Doric colonnade was maintained, but its use marked an important departure in creating interior space. The colonnade arranged in two rows no longer formed three more or less equal aisles; instead the columns were pushed nearer to the walls and were carried around the central area to create a U-shaped portico, ten columns along the sides and five across the back of the hall. Thus was formed a background for the cult statue, a more monumental and appropriate plastic setting.

The success of the formula can be judged from the changes promptly made in the plan of the Temple of Hephaestus then being built on the Kolonos Agoraios, dominating the western edge of the Athenian agora. The foundations of this building show clearly that the arrangement of the interior colonnade was revised in the very process of construction.

The architectural value of the Parthenon is further enhanced by its all-important sculptural decoration. In accordance with the Classical tradition, the pediments and metopes bore sculptures whose themes were taken from the legendary history of Athens and evoke the critical moments of Athena's intervention. The main pediment on the east represented the birth of the goddess, an event quite Parthenonian since she sprang fully armed from the head of Zeus. The other Olympians looked on the scene within their calm, serene world conquered from the giants, whose violent and brutal gestures were to be seen in the metopes beneath the pediment. In these reciprocal scenes were celebrated the victory of intelligence, beauty, and light over the maleficent powers of darkness; the chariot of the sun, in the angle of the pediment, emerged from the sea to displace the chariot of Selene, the moon goddess, whose eclipse at the opposite angle was part of the same symbolism.

The meaning of the great building was already clear to the pilgrim from his inspection of the scene in the west pediment, the contest between Athena and Poseidon for Attica; the two gods finally combined their powers in the alliance of the olive tree and the sea, the two sources of Athenian wealth. The onlookers were the legendary families of Cecrops and Erechtheus, whose very tombs lay close at hand on the sacred rock, here enthroned amid their descendants. The geographical limits were set by the waters that made Athens fruitful: the Cephisus and Eridanus rivers on the north, the Ilissus River and the Callirrhoe fountain on the south.

In the subdued light of the ambulatory Phidias unrolled a frieze around the upper wall, the greatest paean ever sung by the Athenian people in honor of its patron goddess. Phidias himself contributed to the homage of the great procession of the Panathenaic maidens that honored her every four years. Caught in the youthful agitation of departure, the procession started off from the west portico, a natural focus of attention for the pilgrim, and proceeded along the north and south sides of the cella. In spite of the conspicuous

134. *Olympia, sculpture of west pediment, Battle of Lapiths and Centaurs, from Temple of Zeus. Olympia, Museum.*

135. *Olympia, sculpture of east pediment, Contest between Pelops and Oenamaus, from Temple of Zeus. Olympia, Museum.*

presence of city magistrates and the citizenry in general, the accent is on the Athenian youth: the ephebes on horseback, the arrephores carrying the peplos, the maidens, the youths bearing amphoras. At the southeast and northwest corners the divided stream converged on the east portico where the gods were gathered to welcome the Athenian people, whose privileged destiny was thus made manifest to all. Architecture and sculpture, symbolism and realism here find their perfect balance.

After the Parthenon, it was difficult to make innovations. The lessons of the two great masters were not misunderstood, however, and the alliance of styles, like that of disciplines, was still to produce a number of original works that successfully combined the two characteristic aspects of the second period of Classical architecture: the organization of interior space, and the development of decorative structures. Both aspects favored the extension of the Ionic style within exterior colonnades that remained faithful to the strict rules of the Doric order.

Attic architects continued to use Ionic forms with discretion. The Temple of Poseidon on the rocky promontory of Sunium and the Temple of Nemesis at Rhamnus were more slender in proportion, had moldings in the entablature or at the base of the walls and more luxuriant painted decoration, but these minor changes left the Doric structures essentially intact. A different situation developed in the Peloponnesus, where the intrusion of the Ionic style produced a distinct clash between the exterior Doric colonnades and the treatment of the interior; the interiors became completely autonomous and independent. The Temple of Apollo at Bassae illustrates this new conception. Ought we to believe Pausanias when he attributes it to Ictinus? The novel form may indeed have been conceived by the Athenian architect, but the execution was certainly left to local teams whose technique remained traditional and rather clumsy. The plan bears traces of a certain archaism expressed in its elongated proportions (48 by 126 feet, 6 by 15 columns), in the depth of its pronaos, and in the rather spare style of the exterior order. But the interior stems from a totally new approach; the columns, Ionic and Corinthian, bore an entablature with a scuptured marble frieze and a limestone cornice. This was architectonically unrelated with the exterior structure, since the ceiling and the roof framing rested on the walls of the cella; the Ionic system below was merely applied as independent ornament. Thus, the main hall was fringed with Ionic half columns attached to the ends of spur walls, but the back was closed off by flanking Ionic half columns and a single Corinthian column, the earliest known example of that order in all of Greek architecture. The Ionic capitals with their broad volutes were modified to suit their unusual situation; the channel that links the volutes was given a quite strong curvature to accentuate the supporting function. The limestone architrave was embellished with sleek moldings (cyma reversa and cavetto); these merged into the sculptured marble frieze, the whole being crowned by a limestone cornice. Beyond the Corinthian column lay a second smaller hall of uncertain

136. *Athens, Acropolis, view from northwest.*
137. *Athens, plan of Acropolis (from Charbonneaux-Martin-Villard, 1969).*
138. *Athens, Acropolis, Sacred Way, Propylaea, and south wall, from southwest.*
139. *Athens, Acropolis, west facade of Parthenon, seen from Propylaea.*

136. *Athens, Acropolis, view from northwest.*
137. *Athens, plan of Acropolis (from Charbonneaux-Martin-Villard, 1969).*

1. Temple of Atrhena Nike
2. Propylaea / 3. Erechtheion / 4. Temple of Athena / 5. Parthenon

138. *Athens, Acropolis, Sacred Way, Propylaea, and south wall, from southwest.*
139. *Athens, Acropolis, west facade of Parthenon, seen from Propylaea.*

function, its independence emphasized by the unusual presence of a door that opened on the north. Was this a survival of the primitive adyton? or perhaps the mark of a cella, transformed in the course of construction?

Again in Arcadia, Scopas of Paros, an architect and sculptor, clothed the same idea a few years later in a more elaborate and harmonious form in the Temple of Athena Alea at Tegea, having been commissioned to design both the temple and its sculptured decoration. For the exterior Scopas followed tradition by adopting an elongated plan (6 by 14 columns), with the normal distance between cella and peristyle and a wider spacing of the columns in the facade; in the proportions he respected the fourth-century preference for subtler lines, more continuous voids, slimmer columns, and a lighter entablature. The marble afforded greater possibilities than limestone, and it was in the interior that Scopas' creativeness found full expression. He deliberately suppressed the cella colonnades and cross walls, transforming them into an engaged order attached to the wall so as to liberate the entire volume of the cella. Moreover, to accentuate the decorative values he used throughout the Corinthian order, an extremely luxuriant capital composed of a basket of acanthus leaves with vigorously modeled stems and folioles, all in high relief. The Corinthian half columns stood on a plinth decorated with a strong Lesbian molding to set off the Classical profiles of the bases; they supported a slightly projecting band forming the architrave on which, according to the most probable reconstruction, rested another small engaged order, doubtless Ionic, consisting of pilasters or half columns. The religious architecture of the fourth century was thus crystallized in its definitive form.

These characteristics reappear with a few variations in most of the temples and sanctuaries of the period. The mixing of styles became the rule, the development of the decoration a primary concern. The famous and mysterious Tholos of Epidaurus, called Thymele in the building accounts found nearby, bears splendid witness to the new taste—due in large part to the collaboration of architects and sculptors, unless the same artist performed both functions, as Scopas had done. The circular monument was built during the last third of the fourth century to the glory of Asclepius, the healing god; it is a masterpiece of decorative architecture, of the period preceding the excesses of the Hellenistic age. Erected on an artificial mound about ten feet high, the tholos was ringed by twenty-six Doric columns, surely very slim, since the ratio of height (22 feet 6 inches) to the diameter at the base (3 feet 3 inches) was 6:82, close to Hellenistic values. The architrave and frieze, like the columns, were in limestone; the metopes were decorated with large rosettes in a refined style; upon a center in the form of an omphalos unfolded two calyxes of twelve petals each, and among them entwined twelve lotus flowers borne on a long bulbous stem. The conical roof, tiled with marble and bordered by a gutter enriched with foliated scrolls, was topped by an extraordinary finial formed of palmettes and twisted scrolls that emerged from a basket of acanthus leaves; the whole must

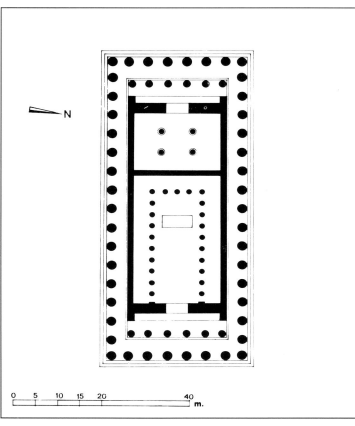

144. Athens, Acropolis, south colonnade and cella wall, Parthenon.

have been ten feet tall. All this heralded the floral repertory displayed in the other parts of the building and associated with the natural polychromy of the materials and with the Corinthian order employed for the interior colonnade. The ceiling of the peristyle, of Pentelic marble, and the cella door are models of architectural elements enhanced even functionally by traditional motifs intelligently adapted. In the cella the fourteen Corinthian columns, also of Pentelic marble, stand out from a stylobate of black stone. The capitals became the first of a long line: the bell is composed of two tiers of eight acanthus leaves each, from which spring the volutes with deeply hollowed stalks that supported the angles of the abacus; in the intervening space is a central volute terminated by a flower with wide-open petals.

The Tholos of Epidaurus comes at the end of a long process of evolution that permitted the combining, in an unstable equilibrium, of decorative elements and architectural structures. It marks the beginning of a swing toward an architecture in which the functional elements are increasingly submerged beneath a flood of decoration.

CIVIC ARCHITECTURE

The brilliance and splendor of Greek temples tend to overshadow the originality of parallel achievements in civic architecture. This is unfortunate, for the civic buildings reflect the development of the political community, the most original feature of ancient Greece.

The early city structures are scarcely distinguishable from the elementary forms of domestic architecture and have no special historical importance. The first buildings intended specifically to house the political and administrative agencies of the *polis* appeared in the sixth century.

The origins of the agora are dealt with in greater detail in the following chapter, on the organization of space; here, we shall consider only the building types that illustrate the particular aspect of this architecture for meetings and assemblies: the prytaneum or town hall, the council hall or Bouleuterion, and the theater.

The prytaneum was at the very heart of the city, the home of the inner council. Its structure was dictated by its function. It sheltered the heart of the city and the cult of the goddess Hestia; it was a repository for the most precious archives; and it provided for communal living imposed on the magistrates, or prytaneis, during their term of office. As so often in the life of the citizen of ancient Greece, the religious and the secular were closely associated. The best examples of this building type are preserved at Priene, Megara Hyblaea, and Delos. Rectangular in plan, it consisted of a sequence of three rooms: the chapel of Hestia; the dining room where the prytaneis or foreign ambassadors and privileged guests of the city ate their meals; and the archives. These rooms opened on a court bordered by one or two porticoes, and by the facade itself; this was more or less monumental in

character, with a light colonnade or propylon, and was closely connected with the agora.

A citizen assembly met in the open air, before it obtained facilities such as the Athenian Pnyx, or was admitted to the theater; but the Boule, or advisory council, had had buildings of its own since the sixth century. The evolution of the Bouleuterion illustrates the progressive conquest of interior space, from which the temples gradually profited. The early examples of a Bouleuterion remained captive to the rectangular plan, ill-adapted to a semicircular seating arrangement; at Delphi and Olympia the ruins show simple, workaday rooms with the councillors' benches ranged along the walls on either side of a central aisle—a system adopted by the Roman Curia and revived centuries later in the British House of Commons. In sixth-century Athens, on the west side of the agora an Athenian architect attempted to reconcile a semicircular seating arrangement with a rectangular plan; the porticoed facade, flanked by a fountain, was eclipsed by neighboring structures. The experiment was not followed up, and the square plan was used in subsequent efforts.

It is important to mention here the influence exerted by the Telesterion, the great hall of mysteries at Eleusis and scene of the initiation ceremonies in the sanctuary of Demeter, especially because the name of Ictinus, the architect of the Parthenon, marks a decisive phase of its evolution. At the beginning of the sixth century the primitive holy place, a rectangular megaron of the Mycenaean type, was incorporated into a great hall with a double interior colonnade, still elongated in plan and little different from contemporary temples. It was about 525 B.C., following the intervention of the Pisistratids, that the critical transition took place, from a rectangular to a square plan. A large square hall (89 by 89 feet) was lined on three sides with tiers of benches (interrupted only in the southeast corner, where part of the original megaron was respected); the east facade had three entrances emphasized by a long portico; the interior space was divided into several aisles by five rows of five columns each, the outer ones abutting the bottom row of benches. This solution was awkward, for the closeness of the columns and their contact with the benches interfered with the sight lines and prevented the spectators from following the ceremonies taking place in the middle of the floor. After Cimon's architects had tried, around 470 B.C., to enlarge the hall and create a central focus out of the primitive sanctuary, it remained for Ictinus to devise the optimal solution. Ictinus took up the same principle but he concentrated, as in the Parthenon, upon freeing the interior space. In the new enlarged hall (170 by 163 feet) the convergence on the center was better defined by the tiers of benches, arranged around all four sides and enclosing the space; passages in three sides, north, south, and east, permit easier circulation. The seven rows of seven columns that featured in Cimon's plan were replaced by twenty columns arranged in two concentric squares; these reinforced the centripetal effect of the composition, freed the sight lines, and gave all the spectators a better view, since

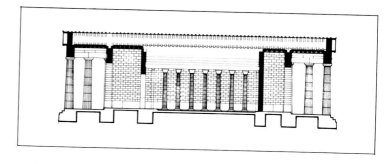

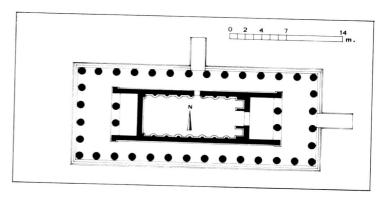

the interval between columns measured more than thirty-three feet, a distance equivalent to the widest interior span of the Parthenon.

This was the first great hall in Greek architecture, and it would be interesting to know more about the design of the structure that covered it; surely it was calculated to enhance the artistic value of the ensemble. In addition, the traditional concerns of an architecture that remained highly sensitive to the balance of volumes, and to the relationship of the building to its environment, are reflected in the exterior porticoes that were to be added to Ictinus' monument on three sides, though this colonnade was never realized. The present state of the Eleusinian hall still retains the broad principles established by Ictinus, but during the fourth century the number of interior columns was again increased and the Archaic portico was simply resumed on the east facade.

Not until the Hellenistic epoch did Ictinus' solution find its full application in vast structures such as the hypostyle hall of Delos. But ruins as well as written records preserve the memory of other square structures, public halls built for political assemblies or spectacles and designed with Classical restraint on a scale appropriate to contemporary cities. Several are preserved in Asia Minor, at Notium, Nysa, and Priene. The Ekklesiasterion, for the Assembly of citizens at Priene (late fourth century), is the most accomplished and best-balanced example. Square in plan, on the north it was built into the hillside and opened on the south through the long portico with a double colonnade that formed the border of the agora; there was access to the assembly hall through two doors that had an exedra between. In the center of the floor, which was free of columns, stood an altar. Tiers of benches surrounded the three sides of the hall opposite the doors. Between each topmost tier and the wall there was space for a narrow gallery, and these contained the pillars that supported the roof (five on the east and west, six on the north). The original span across the hall was about forty-nine feet; subsequently, this had to be reduced at the expense of the central space. Four flights of steps, at the north and south ends of each lateral bank of benches, enabled the Assemblymen to reach their seats.

Another utilitarian building whose layout was closely adapted to its function was the Arsenal of the Piraeus, built by Philo and known from an inscription. Over 100 yards long, it was conceived as a monumental gallery linking the naval dockyard and the agora; the central hall was thus a public thoroughfare, open to the citizens, who could glimpse on either side, beyond the rows of pillars, the sails and tackle of the fleet entrusted to the care of the magistrates; this equipment was stored against the walls and in small lofts, and bore witness to Athenian sea power. A very handsome roof, with strong but simple lines, enhanced the monumentality of the Arsenal, whose external appearance was rather severe despite the Doric frieze that crowned the bare walls. It is a fine example of Classical architecture whose beauty derives from the strict composition dictated by its function.

Though these Greek buildings are not as famous as the temples, they

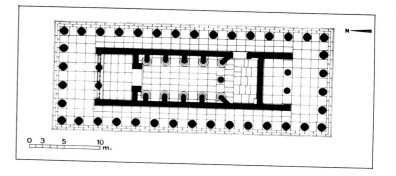

show better their architects' skill in organizing interior space. This mastery is found before or at the same date as the great complexes of the Orient, Egypt, and Rome, all expressing a different spirit and permitting technical developments to which the Greeks did not resort.

The Greek theater never lost its intimate relationship with the terrain and did not become an autonomous building, despite its antiquity as an institution. Religious in origin, political and social in function, the literary works of Aeschylus, Sophocles, and Euripides could not be separated from the role they played within the city nor confined within walls; they were too closely associated with open-air festivals and popular assemblies. At first no more than a level space reserved for dances and ceremonial choruses, the theatral area had no architectural pretensions; spectators clustered on the surrounding slopes or possibly occupied some sort of temporary wooden grandstands.

The theater did not assume a definitive architectural form until the fourth century, when stone tiers of seats, arranged in a semicircle, partially enclosed the orchestra, where the chorus evolved the action of the drama. The actors performed on a low platform in front of the facade for the scenic structure; scenery was strictly schematic, a matter of wings and coulisses. The theater achieved architectural monumentality only in the Hellenistic age.

THE ORGANIZATION OF SPACE AND ARCHITECTURAL COMPOSITION

The evolution of the peripteral temple with its steadily unfolding external colonnade is direct evidence of the sense for volumes and plasticity naturally possessed by the Greek architect, whose situation and aesthetic concerns were no different from those of the sculptor. It is hardly surprising, therefore, that architects very quickly sensed the value of the rapport between architecture and landscape, and among the buildings themselves in the space surrounding them; thus they sought to organize the space within which they placed their structures. But the trends that can be discerned throughout Archaic and Classical times never became strict rules or laws; and although such trends sometimes reflected certain mathematical, even geometric preoccupations, neither were they a matter of pure aesthetics. Social and economic conditions, the political structure of the city, and the evolution of philosophical speculation—all these at one time or another exerted influence on the organization of space within the urban setting where the great works of architecture were erected. The outcome was a considerable degree of diversity. Each region of the Greek world and, indeed, each city developed its own variants according to its particular social or political circumstances. Our aim here is to be aware of nuances, and not to formulate the precepts of a code but to pursue the great trends that express the various aspects of the life and history of the Greek city.

The first and oldest concern was to individualize the abode of the god.

155. Bassae, interior of cella, Temple of Apollo, from south.

156. Bassae, Pronaos, Temple of Apollo, from north.

157. Segesta, Doric temple seen from theater hill, on southeast.

The Greek countryside offered its own resources, but it was also necessary to integrate and adapt the temple with the lines of the landscape. In this task came the first success. Whether the temple stood on the summit of a hill (as at Aegina) or on a terrace carefully differentiated from its rolling surroundings (Bassae, Rhamnus, Segesta, the Argive Heraion, Delphi), whether it terminated a promontory (Sunium, Croton, Panionion, Notium), dominated or enframed a cityscape (Athens, Acragas, Paestum), or was spread over the back of a valley or on a seashore (Samos, Didyma, Claros, Caulonia, the Heraion of Paestum), the temple always preserved its individuality, stole into the landscape while developing or complementing the natural lines. There is no need to elaborate on a rule so consistently respected.

There were problems, however, variously solved by resorting to diverse architectural elements, and having implications that extend far beyond the boundaries of the sanctuary. We will examine them in turn, studying the relations between the principal building and associated structures in the same complex; the organization of space and its utilization in architectural ensembles, sanctuaries, or public places; and finally the links between architectural groupings and the urban setting whose tendencies or deep-seated characteristics they express.

Relations Among Individual Buildings

Whether it is a sanctuary comprising several buildings or a public place collecting the elements necessary to the public life of the city, functional considerations are the key to composition.

In the Archaic sanctuaries the temple, the house of the deity, is isolated and sharply individualized, but nonetheless closely related with the altar, the place of sacrifice, which was outside but not far away. Ritual necessities led to the erection of the altar in an arrangement that quickly became standardized, opposite to the facade of the temple and often linked with it by a paved path. There were numerous variants, more often attributable to the ritual forms of a cult rather than to purely aesthetic considerations. It should not be forgotten that the faithful had to be able to follow the sacrificial ceremonies, to participate in the processions that wound through the sanctuary, and to accompany the cult statue when, on festive occasions, it left the temple to be shown publicly—sometimes, after certain purification rites, to be exposed to the gaze of the faithful.

The first attempts at composition were associated with the development of the separate monumental entrance, the propylon. Whatever its location with respect to the temple, it disclosed the latter from an angle chosen with the more or less explicit intention of displaying it to best effect. It is worth noting that, from the outset, the architects avoided a frontal or axial disclosure; the building is progressively revealed, and along oblique or diagonal lines. The sanctuaries of Athena on Aegina, the early structures on Delos, the path that had to be followed by pilgrims to the Heraion of

access to the sacred plateau through five gates pierced through a cross wall that cut off the corridor between two lateral ramparts. However, a slight difference in orientation brought the axis of the new building into relation with the point of arrival of the Sacred Way and with the east-west axis of the plateau separating the Parthenon from the Erechtheion. To acknowledge and emphasize the ascending motion of the procession, the central block of the new Propylaea with its five doors was sited where the break in the western slope was most abrupt, on a five-step substructure that compensates for the difference in level between the front and back thresholds. The continuity of movement was underscored by the superior proportions of the central western gate (13 feet 8 inches wide, 24 feet 4 inches tall), and the smooth ramp that replaced the steps to facilitate the passage of the chariot of the goddess; the central bay of the portico in front of it is correspondingly enlarged (nearly 18 feet wide, as opposed to 12 feet for the lateral bays). An approaching procession was greeted by a facade of six Doric columns springing from a four-step crepidoma, which projected at a right angle on either side to support the colonnades of the lateral facades that framed the broad platform of the entrance.

The problem, however, was how to arrange the way of access into the vestibule behind the portico. It was here that a correspondence was established with the Parthenon, the main building of the sanctuary; the width of the vestibule (60 feet) approximates that of the principal cella of the Parthenon, and the depth (42 feet) that of the Parthenon's western cella. Moreover, the Ionic order supporting the ceiling of the cella was adopted, by Mnesicles for the vestibule, which thus became a sort of prelude to the composition of Ictinus. Bordering the axial corridor that ascended toward the great central opening, Mnesicles placed two rows of three Ionic columns each, whose slenderness surpasses all Classical and Hellenistic norms. The aisles were covered by coffered marble ceilings whose marble beams were almost twenty feet long. Here, Mnesicles had to resort to an unusual technique in order to reinforce the Ionic architraves that held up the ceiling—he inserted metal bars. As the pilgrim finally emerged into the east portico, he was confronted with the two unequal and asymmetrical masses—the Parthenon to the south and the Erechtheion to the north—on either side of the median axis marked by votive shrines and isolated statues or groups of statuary. The details of the composition and decoration of each monument were only progressively revealed to him. The first glimpse of the mighty volume of the Parthenon was from an oblique angle, encompassing the Propylaea's sharply defined east facade and the Parthenon's receding north colonnade. One can only conclude that the concept of axiality was systematically spurned and the possibilities of symmetry deliberately rejected.

With variations dictated by landscape and site, the same concerns are equally apparent in complexes as different as Delos and Olympia. And at Delphi the pilgrim who mounted the Sacred Way at the foot of the

Samos or the Altis at Olympia, the first sanctuary on the acropolis of Selinus—all offer excellent illustrations of this concern, expressed with ultimate refinement by Attic architects on the Athenian acropolis.

In the Propylaea Mnesicles acknowledged the subtleties introduced by Callicrates and Ictinus in designing the Parthenon. While duly respecting the individuality of the two buildings separated by an interval of some ten years' time, the architect closely coordinated their relative positions in space and their mathematical proportions. One feels a growing admiration for the skill of Mnesicles, placing his building in the most difficult topographical site and inventing handsome architectural forms to accommodate the various functions of the edifice. Forbidden to infringe on the sanctuary of Athena Nike to the southwest, confined on the south by the sacred precincts of Artemis, and obliged to incorporate a portion of the sixth-century propylaea and to accommodate on the west the twists and turns of the Sacred Way (the route followed by the procession with its chariots and sacrificial animals), Mnesicles succeeded in designing a building that accepts these multiple constraints yet still achieves a profound and genuine unity. He respected the fundamental rhythm of the Archaic propylaea, which gave

161. Sunium, Temple of Poseidon, from north.

Phaedriades discovered progressively from one level to the next the ex-votos dedicated to Apollo, all placed at different angles. Leaving behind the groups of sculpture that adorned the approaches, he skirted the Treasury of the Sicyonians, noting the back of the Treasury of the Siphnians (its sumptuous facade, with its caryatids, revealing itself only at the turning of the path), at which point the Treasury of the Athenians was already in full view. As he continued upward he saw, beyond the Athenian Stoa and over the polygonal terrace-wall, the top of the colonnades of the main Temple of Apollo; its facade as well as the long north flank would come into view only as he emerged at the northeast corner of the esplanade, after rounding the back of the great blue limestone Apollo Altar of Chios. He was then in the heart of the sanctuary, which had revealed itself to him gradually, from a variety of angles.

Without occupying the geometric center or playing the part of a controlling element, the Temple of Zeus at Olympia dominated the lines of colonnades that accompanied the steps of the pilgrim entering the compound at the northwest corner. From this point the temple can be instantly apprehended, first the west facade and the long north flank, which one had to skirt before contemplating the pediment of the main facade, where Zeus presided over the historic race in which Pelops won both the hand of Hippodamia and power over Elis. Even the processions of the competitors in the Olympic Games followed a winding path among various colonnades until, at the foot of the Terrace of the Treasuries, they reached the gateway of the stadium, flanked by embankments where the spectators gathered.

In all these instances one can discern the same principles linking the buildings in indefinite and fluid relationships. One volume is played off against the other, but not in the strict lines of geometric composition. Only in the following epoch did Hellenistic architects, under other influences, fall back upon axiality and symmetry for organizing their vast building projects.

THE ORGANIZATION OF SPACE WITHIN ARCHITECTURAL COMPLEXES

The functional relationships among buildings associated in the same complex, whether sanctuary or public square, came to determine the principles that controlled their grouping in space.

First we notice the definite contours that delimited the reserved area; these grew from the sacredness of such zones. The sanctuary constituted a temenos, a word whose etymology implies a particular sector dedicated to a divinity. An enclosure, materialized in the form of a wall or merely indicated by boundary markers, limited the extent of construction. The same was true of the marketplace or agora, which belonged to the public domain and formed a zone protected by religious sanctions. These sacred bounds

119

162. Sunium, trabeation, southeast
corner of Temple of Poseidon.
163. Sunium, south side of Temple
of Poseidon.

162. Sunium, trabeation, southeast
corner of Temple of Poseidon.

163. Sunium, south side of Temple
of Poseidon.

required a definite architectural composition that could not dissolve into an indetermined area. As early as the eighth and seventh centuries one can discern these characteristics in sites as far apart as, for example, the sanctuary of Hera on Samos and the agora of Megara Hyblaea in Sicily. One can follow the formation of the main sanctuary on the acropolis of Selinus a century later, for the procedures are the same: to give the contours of the sacred zone a more definite structure, the simple boundary wall was gradually replaced by the portico, its colonnade originally in wood.

The first known stoa at Samos, the south stoa, ran behind the temple and along the edge of the sanctuary; its wooden posts have disappeared, but the stone bases remain. About the middle of the seventh century the agora of Megara Hyblaea recalls the same arrangement; the marketplace was separated from the surrounding streets and quarters toward north and east by two simple stoas opening on the square. In the next century the stoa on the acropolis of Selinus, as at Samos, had two wings joined at a right angle, accentuating the function of the porticoes.

Not only did stoas enclose and accurately delimit space, they also provided a decorative motif; they formed a background that set off the principal structures—the temple and its altar, or the main buildings of the agora—while providing refuge and shelter for pilgrims and citizens. The usefulness of these porticoes led to their rapid proliferation. The large covered areas at the Athenian agora and in the sanctuary of Artemis Brauronia in Attica had been converted by the end of the fifth century into rooms or shops for administrative or religious functions.

There was no stopping the development of this major architectural theme as it adapted itself to new sites and purposes. A further advance was registered in the fifth century when the L-shaped stoa was given one more wing so that it now enclosed space on three sides. The first example was apparently the stoa of the sanctuary of Artemis at Brauron on the northeast coast of Attica. In this sanctuary, a sort of monastery where young Athenian girls lived as acolytes of Artemis, a little temple with a sacred spring was built on the south, against the rocky cliff. The sanctuary extended to the north, and consisted of a U-shaped portico whose central building communicated with an interior court and another parallel structure where the offerings were stored. Beyond the north and west colonnades there were rooms whose furnishings indicate their purpose: here the servants of the goddess took their communal meals. The temple, offset in relation to the axis of the porticoes, closed a composition organized around a carefully delimited space.

Within zones thus defined the buildings could be arranged with considerable freedom. In the sanctuaries the temple served as a center of attraction for the ex-votos which customarily lined the sacred way, or were placed in a circle around the temple esplanade when the nature of the site permitted. At Delos the treasuries built in the sixth and fifth centuries were distributed in a semicircle around the sacred enclave occupied by the three

temples of Apollo; whereas the offerings connected with the Temple of Artemis in the area more exactly defined by the L-shaped stoa of the Naxians, were arranged around that esplanade and along the sacred way leading from the harbor. This dual principle is equally evident at Samos. The temple, associated with the altar and the enclosure around the sacred tree of Hera, formed the principal mass, and was freely surrounded by small shrines dedicated to the deity. Other chapels and pedestals bordered the sacred way. These progressive and rather random groupings reflected the living evolution of the sanctuaries, and also the complexity and disparity of the secondary cults that were often associated with the worship of the principal deity.

Agora buildings were also grouped according to a functional principle. The first clear example, as we have seen, is afforded by Megara Hyblaea in the mid-seventh century, when the city became organized on a definite plan. Stoas formed the boundaries of the trapezoidal marketplace at north and east. On the south two rectangular temples, without peristyles, were laid out along one line; the connections with the quarters adjacent to the square remained ill-defined. The west side lay along one of the great arteries of the city, beyond which stood a row of public buildings of a civic or religious character. Passing from north to south, one encounters sanctuaries where the finds (*bothroi*, tablets with cupules) suggest heroic cults, then an anonymous building, and then a complex within which the plan of a prytaneum is clearly discernible.

At the beginning of the sixth century the reforms of Solon had given positive direction toward a democratic regime in the city of Athens, where the architectural framework was created that symbolized its form of government and welcomed the first organizations needed for its functioning. The agora was detached from the acropolis. Along its western edge, at the foot of the Kolonos Agoraios, there arose as at Megara a row of religious and political buildings: the first sanctuary of Zeus Agoraios, the temples of Apollo and Demeter, the Bouleuterion, and the first Prytaneum that preceded the Tholos. This was a disorderly succession of buildings with dissimilar plans, which later caused a great deal of trouble when Hellenistic taste insisted upon the regularization of the colonnaded facades. The limits of public land reserved for the agora were fixed by boundary markers, several of which have been found in their original positions. During the fifth and fourth centuries the contours of the square were regularized, and girded with the succession of civic and religious buildings. On the northeast, on the north, and to the south, utilitarian stoas were erected to house the offices, meeting places, tribunals, and picture galleries where mythical and historical achievements of the city were celebrated. The ruins, as excavated by the American School of Classical Studies, confirm that the Athenian agora was not organized on any systematic principle, but simply performed the multiple functions of a public square and a symbol of Athenian democracy. The testimony of Demosthenes, in the second half of the fourth century,

169. *Epidaurus, interior corridors in
foundations of Tholos.*

170. *Epidaurus, section of Tholos
(from Roux, 1961).*

171. *Epidaurus, plan of Tholos
(from Roux, 1961).*

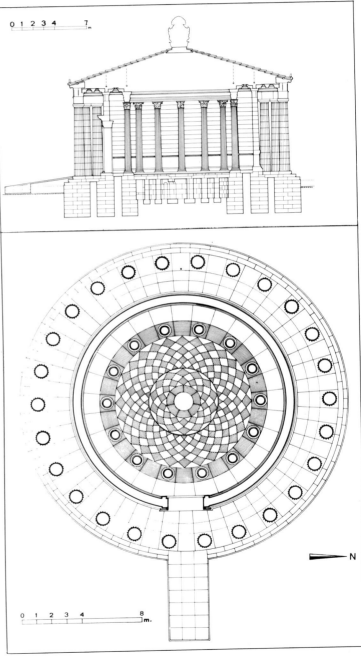

172. *Epidaurus, reconstructed section, including wall and trabeation of Tholos. Epidaurus, Museum.*

173. *Epidaurus, Corinthian capital from interior of Tholos. Epidaurus, Museum.*

174. *Eleusis, plans showing evolution of Telesterion (from Charbonneaux-Martin-Villard, 1969).*

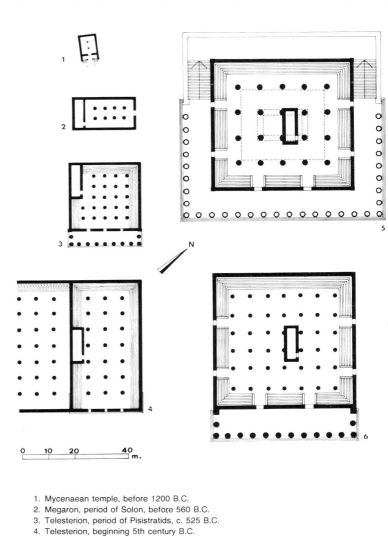

1. Mycenaean temple, before 1200 B.C.
2. Megaron, period of Solon, before 560 B.C.
3. Telesterion, period of Pisistratids, c. 525 B.C.
4. Telesterion, beginning 5th century B.C.
5. Telesterion, Ictinus, mid 5th century B.C.
6. Telesterion, final solution, 4th century B.C.

graphically evokes its teeming life and colorful complexity (Oration XVIII, 169): "It was evening, and one had come to the Prytanes with the news that Elateia had been taken [by Philip of Macedon]. Upon this they rose up from supper without delay; some of them drove the occupants out of the booths in the market place and set fire to the wicker-work; others sent for the generals and summoned the trumpeter; and the city was full of commotion."

THE RELATIONS BETWEEN ARCHITECTURAL COMPLEXES AND THE URBAN FRAMEWORK: THE BIRTH OF GREEK CITY-PLANNING

Closely linked with the political and social structure of the Greek city, the architectural complexes of sanctuaries, agoras, and gymnasia could not be detached from the urban framework that formed the core of the political community; in particular the Hellenic conception of the *polis,* the city-state, required autonomy and independence for all the institutions that made it unique. Thus the city left its mark on the shaping of the principles of architectural composition.

These principles and interrelationships depended, however, upon the historical conditions that had kept alive the evolution of the city-state. In the ancient cities progressive transformations brought about the traditional succession of regimes as defined by Plato: monarchy rooted in Mycenaean traditions, then the oligarchy or aristocracy of the great landowners, and finally democracy, which initiated the redistribution of wealth and the importance of expanded trade. The acropolis, site of the royal palace, was associated with the temple of the protective god; together they dominated the city and formed its monumental crown. The agora, endowed with public buildings and serving commercial functions, was a later development, situated in the new city and oriented outward, toward the ports.

Athens is a good example of the ancient type of urban growth, Miletus of the later. In this planned type the urban land is divided to conform with the social and economic functions of the city, and then into lots determined by a more or less regular grid; within this system the most important architectural features are allocated the privileged sites. It is important to realize that Athens and Miletus reacted in quite different ways at about the same time and under more or less comparable historical conditions. In 494 B.C. the Persians razed Miletus and drove out its inhabitants; in 480 they invaded Athens, burned the buildings on the acropolis, and set fire to part of the town: when the two cities began the work of reconstruction, Athens remained faithful to the ancient system, but Miletus opted unreservedly for geometrism, for the rectangular system.

Athens clung to its acropolis, once the site of the royal palace and of the legendary family of the Cecropes but now entirely reserved for the worship of the gods. We know from the records that the agora was situated in Archaic

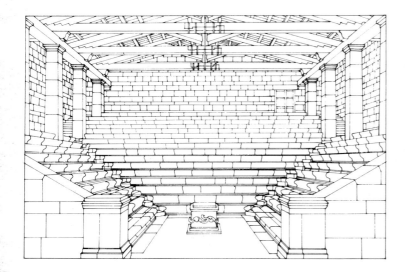

178. Priene, reconstruction of ekklesiasterion (from Schede, 1964).

179. Priene, view of agora.

180. Priene, theater, from north.

181. *Piraeus, reconstruction of
Arsenal (from Lawrence, 1957).*
182. *Piraeus, section of Arsenal
(from Lawrence, 1957).*

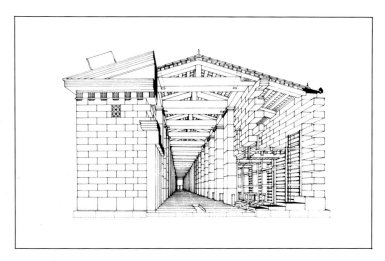

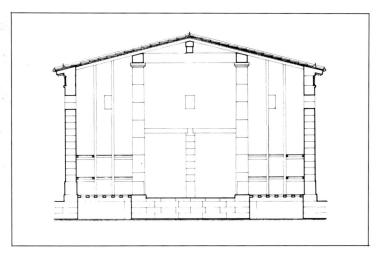

times on the low western slopes of the acropolis, almost at the foot of the Mycenaean fortifications that are still preserved at several points. The city itself developed along the adjacent valley between the Areopagus and the Pnyx, and to the south, the area to the north being occupied by necropolises; it was a narrow, cramped city with winding streets, clinging to the skirts of the isolated sacred rock with its own buildings on top. The break came at the beginning of the sixth century, with Solon and his social reforms; the agora was transferred to the site of the ancient necropolises, between the fortified zone of the acropolis and the new quarters of the artisans and merchants. The old roads formed the axes along which the various buildings were distributed: the north-south thoroughfare, defined toward the close of the sixth century by boundary markers reading "I am where the agora ends," fronted the administrative and religious side (Prytaneum, Bouleuterion, and cults of Demeter, Apollo Patroos, Zeus Phratrios, Zeus Agoraios); the square was crossed diagonally, from northwest to southeast, by the Panathenaic Way, whose path remained unchanged through the centuries. The new square received an articulating and communicating role in the city with the Altar of the Twelve Gods, the zero milestone from which distances from Athens were reckoned. In connection with other streets, stoas and buildings were irregularly sited around the edges of the square, with the established traffic patterns scrupulously respected. The Athenian agora exercised no real influence on the city's architecture, and did not become an object of systematic planning until the advent of the Hellenistic age.

It is significant that about the same time, in the years following the victories over the Persians (480-479 B.C.), the Athenians concentrated their first efforts on refortifying the acropolis, then restored the lower city to its traditional appearance. But they rebuilt the Piraeus along entirely new lines, calling in as planner the theoretician Hippodamus. He was then supervising the reconstruction of Miletus, and his name, Hippodamus of Miletus, was to become the symbol of Greek city-planning; more philosopher than architect, he formulated rules derived from his reflections on what would be optimal living conditions for city dwellers, and on the realizations already to be found in the cities of Archaic Greece, particularly in Magna Graecia. Applying these rules to the Piraeus, the space within the city was allocated to various urban functions; administrative, religious, and business zones intercommunicated, and served political, religious, social, and economic interests with buildings adapted to their functions. Each zone considered the property of the state (the *demosion*) was delimited by boundary markers, several of which have been found, some still on the very spots where the ancient surveyors placed them. Thus it has been possible to identify the commercial port zone, the mooring zone, and the boundaries of the agora in relation to the naval dockyard. The agora was connected with the dockyard by the long gallery already mentioned, built in the fourth century by the architect Philo, where the sails and tackle of the Greek navy were stored. The commercial zone, surrounded by great porticoes used as

XVIII. Priene, theater.

185. *Epidaurus, theater, from north.*   186. *Segesta, theater, from southwest.*
187. *Aegosthena, fortified tower.*

188, 189. *Eleutherai, fortification walls with towers.*

190. *Acragas, Temple of Castor and Pollux, Sanctuary of Chthonic Deities, from east.*

warehouses, was linked by a monumental route with the temples and sanctuaries, as well as with the agora. This monumental complex occupied the center of the site, around which extended the residential quarters, in three principal zones.

The growth of modern Piraeus has obscured the architectural lines of the ancient city, though it is well defined in plan by the boundary markers and other sporadic finds. But the excavations at Miletus illustrate the precise architectural forms generated by the Hippodamian planning principles. Within the rectangular grid laid out by the surveyors, a certain number of lots were reserved for public buildings; these were distributed along the two branches of an L-shaped route connecting the two main harbors, separated by the theater promontory. At the meeting point of the two branches was located the principal agora, whose boundaries were sharply defined by great porticoes with rooms; links with the street system were provided at either end of the colonnades. The succession of buildings along the north branch included the Bouleuterion, gymnasia, the sanctuary of Apollo Delphinios, and finally the markets and big warehouses of the large Lion Harbor; to the east lay other markets and the principal sanctuary of the city, that of Athena. The three distinct residential quarters were regularly laid out in blocks.

Stoas and colonnades formed the bony structure of these compositions, defining the boundaries and establishing the orientation of the main axes; they impressed a certain unity on otherwise unrelated structures by combining them in groups behind formally composed facades. Thus the architecture was closely linked with the city plan, an expression of its principles and functions. This plan was realized gradually, and not fully implemented until the end of the Hellenistic epoch, but it had been so firmly conceived that the empty areas were steadily filled in the course of the centuries, with little incentive to depart from it. Moreover, the city fathers were steadfast in imposing the rules, even on princely benefactors, as may be seen from the proscriptions in a decree that required the architects of Antiochus III to conform to the city law when the king offered to build a great stoa for Miletus.

Several centuries before Hippodamus, the origin of the principles can be discovered that the philosophers were later to analyze and impose as rules on their ideal city. Plato drew liberally on the examples offered by the Greek colonies in the west. The excavations at Megara Hyblaea in eastern Sicily, and studies pursued at Camarina, Selinus, Monte Casale, and Metapontum, permit us to reconstruct with some precision the evolution of this urban architecture. Its first manifestations can be found in the seventh century,

194. Paestum, Temple of Hera I (Basilica), from north.

in the urbanizing trend that followed the establishment of Greek colonies in Sicily and southern Italy. The plan of Megara Hyblaea shows that in the middle of the seventh century several main axes created a division of the site of the city with the secondary streets, and defined a space composed of more or less regular blocks, though the layout was not strictly geometric. A public zone was bounded by two east-west axes (though not strictly parallel), by a cross street on the north, and, less definitely, by the siting of two temples on the south. Trapezoidal in plan, the marketplace was separated from the streets that bounded it by stoas designed not to cut the flow of traffic. The north stoa, in particular, had a wide gateway in the middle communicating with the secondary street to the north, which was interrupted by the agora. On the west side the street was incorporated in the square; along its outer edge, beyond the roadway, the buildings were inlaid, as it were, in an otherwise residential block. It is noteworthy that no earlier foundations were uncovered beneath the lowest level of the agora; the agora was part of the original plan, and no structures had to be cleared away to make room for it.

Wherever our study of the Archaic cities of Sicily has revealed the existence of a rational plan, it has proved to be based on the same block principle. At Camarina the primitive nucleus controlled the direction of subsequent growth; at Monte Casale a large part of the plateau was divided by parallel streets branching off the principal axis, which originated on a platform constituting a sort of acropolis. The regular plan of Metapontum goes back in large part to the seventh or early sixth century, and in it one can see the primacy of the sanctuary of the Lycian Apollo and of the agora that doubtless formed its continuation on the east. Inscriptions, recently published, bear witness to the importance of the *horoi,* boundary markers that fixed the limits of the sacred domain, the religious domain, and the zones allocated to the citizens. The acropolis is conspicuously absent from these sites; for the emigrants it stood for a regime from which they had fled. Plans based on a regular partitioning of the land into blocks, permitting space to be reserved immediately for the religious organizations that symbolized both the reality and the aspirations of the new community, were well suited to their political and social requirements. There was no need to defer to ancient eastern traditions; the plan evolved from the conditions themselves and from the exigencies that prevailed at each settlement. This form of urbanization and the principles of architectural composition that followed from it explain the specific characteristics of Greek colonial cities.

Monumental composition was at first subjected to the city plan, but did not long submit to that condition; it was particularly stimulated by the

XIX. *Epidaurus, theater.*

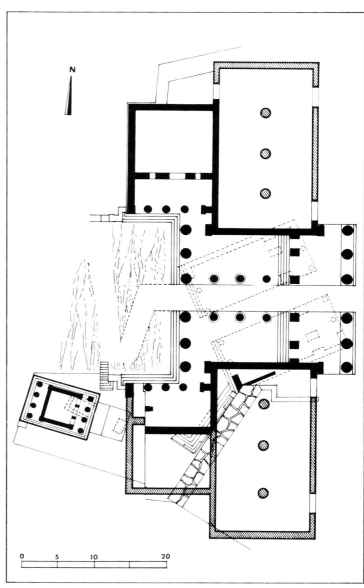

N

0   5   10   20

political and economic development of the colonies. The ambitions of the
tyrants and their desire for ostentation, combined with the financial
resources at their disposal, led to an architectural expansion that burst apart
the original frame. The evolution of the first sanctuary on the acropolis of
Selinus is a good example of this process. The temenos, which enclosed altars
and shrines whose earliest remains are from the seventh century, was laid
out at the intersection of two roads, one linking the acropolis with the city
spread out over the hills to the north, and the other the two ports flanking
the plateau on east and west. Its irregular contours were first recognized
by E. Gabrici and fixed more precisely by M. di Vita. The initial extension
of the terrace toward the east came as early as 570-560 B.C., when the first
great temple, Temple C, was built. During the last quarter of the sixth
century the development of the sanctuary was included in a scheme for the
regularization of the great axes, as part of a vast public works program. A
second temple, Temple D, was added to the complex. On the west and the
south the temenos walls were aligned with the streets; a great terrace was

constructed on the east, stabilized with a massive stepped retaining wall; an L-shaped stoa was erected to define the boundaries of the esplanade, following the principles already seen on Samos. By a sort of reduplication of masses, the temples were to succeed one another to the south, on the acropolis, and still more superbly to the east, where each temple was parallel to the next.

About the same time, toward the end of the sixth century, an almost identical program was initiated at Paestum. A great north-south thoroughfare formed the backbone of the plan; a uniform succession of residential blocks stretched between this axis and the western limits of the site, toward the sea. The main thoroughfare was bordered on the east by the wall of an immense temenos that received the temples of Hera, then the sanctuaries of the agora, and at the north the Temple of Athena. At Acragas the monumental zone was located south of the city, where it could take excellent advantage of a stretch of terrain that dominated the plain on which the city lay. The whole was subtended by a great thoroughfare, which formed the base of the triangle whose apex was to be the acropolis, itself crowned by a sanctuary. Along the road that led westward, to the sanctuary of the chthonian deities, lay the agora, the great Temple of Zeus, and, at some

151

202. *Olympia, vaulted entrance to stadium.*

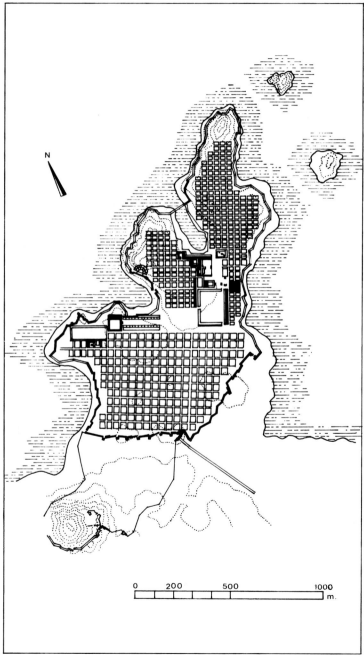

203. *Miletus, plan of city (from Kleiner, 1968).*

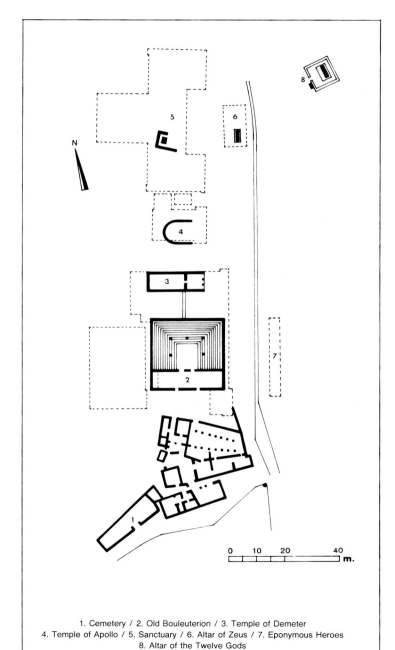

1. Cemetery / 2. Old Bouleuterion / 3. Temple of Demeter
4. Temple of Apollo / 5. Sanctuary / 6. Altar of Zeus / 7. Eponymous Heroes
8. Altar of the Twelve Gods

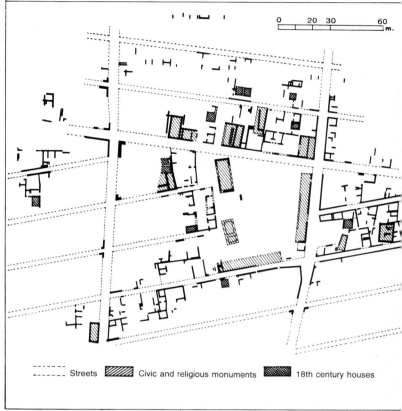

- - - - Streets   ▨ Civic and religious monuments   ▨ 18th century houses

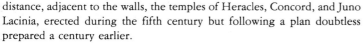

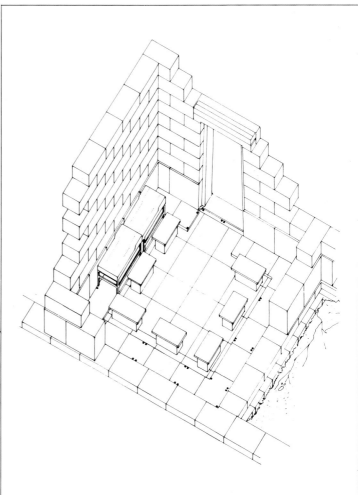

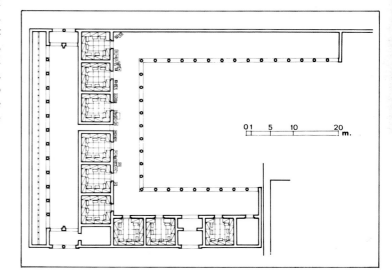

distance, adjacent to the walls, the temples of Heracles, Concord, and Juno Lacinia, erected during the fifth century but following a plan doubtless prepared a century earlier.

Such, then, is the meaning and importance of the great monumental ensembles of Sicily and southern Italy. Today they appear to be isolated, cut off from the cities of which they are the most brilliant ornament. But they should not be seen detached from the urban setting; on the contrary, they are closely linked to it by their function and their architectural prominence. Too important to be squeezed into the compartments of a sometimes constricting rectangular grid, they form, as it were, a backdrop that occasionally has truly theatrical effect, but always they express a sense of proportions and a flare for the art of siting that are rooted in the fundamental traditions of Greek architecture.

209. *Brauron, plan of stoa,*
Sanctuary of Artemis Brauronia (from
Bouras, 1967).

210. *Athens, view of agora, from*
southeast.

Greek architecture of the Hellenistic age gives rise to varied judgments, not all of them favorable. What sometimes deceives us is the degradation of the Classical forms and motifs; these tend to become dry and impoverished and lose their strength and vigor, but in this period one should not overlook the luxuriance and diversity of their many themes. And at the same time the development of the vault and the arcade, the knowing use of engaged orders in decorative compositions, and the variety demanded of sculpture and painting constitute a repertory that is new, or at least much enriched by all the Classical forms. But the originality of Hellenistic architecture is not confined to its formal aspects; these could not compensate for inferior workmanship. The strength of the architects lies in the creative vigor of their monumentality and the amplification of their structures. They adapted the Classical tradition to the new conditions of the Greek world, its geography now vastly extended.

The civic style of architecture yielded to a princely and monarchical architecture; ostentation, political prestige, and a desire to enlist the arts on the side of economic or financial power drastically upset the proportions and balances that the structure of Classical cities had imposed. Let us pause to consider the methods of this architecture before examining its finest achievements, those that furnished later ages with a repertory of forms and structures that were used for several centuries.

The Hellenistic architects, who first built for Alexander and then lavished their skill on the kingdoms of his successors in Asia Minor, Syria, and Egypt (before nurturing the infant architecture of Rome), were not revolutionaries; on the contrary, they were decidedly conservative in their use of forms and motifs.

The traditional orders, Doric and Ionic, continued to live on, but the difficulties inherent in the Doric frieze, as well as the taste for decorative expression, favored the spread of the Ionic style. The most Classical of these architects, Pythius of Priene in the late fourth century and Hermogenes a century later, held forth on the superiority of the Ionic order. Vitruvius preserves an echo of their arguments (*De architectura,* IV, iii, 1): "Some ancient architects have said that temples should not be constructed in the Doric style, because faulty and unsuitable correspondence arose in them; for example Arcesius, Pythius and especially Hermogenes. For the last named after preparing a supply of marble for a temple in the Doric style, changed over, using the same marble, and built an Ionic temple to Father Bacchus [Temple of Dionysus at Teos] not because the form or style or dignity of the plan is displeasing, but because the distribution of the triglyphs and soffits is confused and inconvenient."

The rhythm of the Doric frieze had indeed to satisfy two contradictory requirements. First, the center of each triglyph should coincide with the axis of the column below; this presented no difficulty along a colonnade, but at the corner of the portico two triglyphs were supposed to abut so as to form a neat articulation. This meant the metope must be offset from above

the corner column, and consequently the last metope must be wider than the others. This problem had been evaded since the end of the Archaic period by reducing the width of the last bay of the facade, or, to make the interruption less obtrusive, by dividing this reduction between the last two bays. But this brought necessary changes into proportions at all levels, from the slabs of the crepidoma on which the columns stood, to the blocks of the entablature and the cornices; the consequences became more disturbing when geometric procedures were developed to define the interrelationships among all the elements of the colonnade.

In a system where the discipline of geometry tended to impose rather rigid formulas, the shortening of the corner spans meant a disrespect for symmetry and a want of rhythm that was alien to the very nature of the Doric order. And if to this is added the evolution of forms that made the columns increasingly slender and the lines in general more dry and rigid, and reduced the proportions of the entablature and accentuated its narrowness, then the progressive disappearance of the Doric order from the temples is easy to understand; it continued to be used in the great stoas and long colonnades, where, reduced to aligned facades between the antae of lateral walls, it posed no architectural problem. During the Hellenistic age the Doric order was essentially the order of stoas.

At the same time the Ionic order, whose entablature was free of these shortcomings, was being developed and enriched; moreover, its easy acceptance of decorative motifs commended it to the prevailing taste. With the invention of the angle capital that is square in plan with its four volutes placed on the diagonals, the first known example coming from the Nereid Monument at Xanthos, was solved one of the difficulties associated with the use of the order in the peristyle. Formerly the volutes had been confined to the two principal faces; as the ends displayed only the cushion connecting the spirals, the capital did not meet the requirements of an angle location, to be viewed from both sides, nor did it provide the extra volume that an exposed support needed at the point of intersection of two colonnades. Bases and capitals were given a more vigorous and elaborate ornamentation. In the Temple of Artemis Cybele at Sardis, a fleuron appeared in the center of the channel, above a more vigorous ovolo that is half-concealed by broad palmettes. In the Temple of Apollo at Didyma, figures of gods were applied to the volutes of certain capitals. The two motifs, on the channel and between the volutes, became developed, and the popularity of the historiated capital in the Hellenistic and Roman epochs is well known.

Hellenistic architecture did not invent the Corinthian capital but welcomed it very warmly—at the expense of the Ionic order, retaining only its base and shaft. The origins of the Corinthian style, hidden from the eyes of the ancient historians, remain something of a mystery. According to Pliny, the capital was invented by the Athenian sculptor Callimachus, Phidias' pupil, who is supposed to have been seduced by the sight of an offering basket left on a tomb and enveloped naturally by the leaves of an acanthus

214. *Epidaurus, restoration of Corinthian capital and trabeation from Tholos. Epidaurus, Museum.*

215, 216. *Sarcophagus of the Mourning Women, end reliefs. Istanbul, Archaeological Museum.*

217. *Acragas, restored telamones from Temple of Zeus. Agrigento, Museum.*

218. *Acragas, plan of Temple of Zeus (from Bervé-Gruben, 1962).*

219. *Epidaurus, isometric reconstruction of Temple L (from Roux, 1961).*

220. *Thasos, relief on Gate of Selinus.*

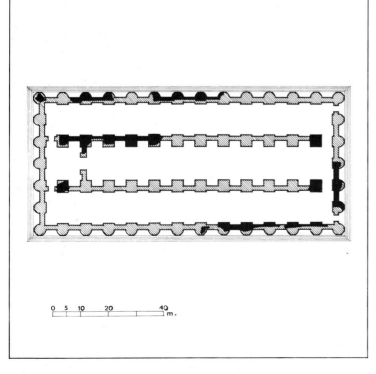

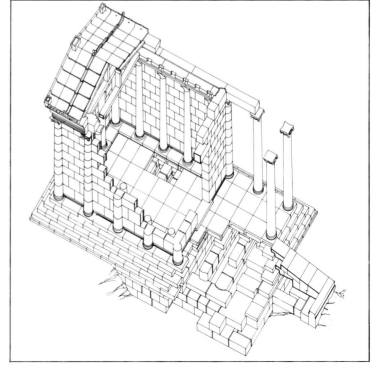

plant that chanced to take root there. The legend, as so often, contains a degree of truth. The origin of the Corinthian capital is doubtless associated with the motif of acanthus leaves so freely used on fifth-century funerary steles, either forming a basket at the base, or replacing the earlier palmette at the top. Representations of the same motif on white-ground funerary lekythoi illustrate the same affiliation.

Furthermore, the motif satisfied the taste for architectural decoration that emerged during the fourth century, and the Corinthian colonnade reflected new developments in organizing interior space where the pillars and columns had architectonic functions as well as decorative ones. The bell covered with acanthus provided a flexible means of adorning a cylindrical capital that was easily adaptable, either in its complete form or as crowning a half column or square pillar, to the various purposes it might serve in the architectural and decorative design of a hall. This is why a Corinthian column occurs in curious association with the Ionic order in the cella of the Temple of Apollo at Bassae.

Subsequently in the Tholos at Delphi it was employed on the columns attached inside the cella wall supporting the roof framing; it flourished vigorously in the hands of the sculptor-architect Scopas at the temple of Tegea, becoming the principal theme of the interior order of half columns of the handsome cella; and it assumed final form in the interior columns of the Tholos of Epidaurus, rising unsuspected behind the severity of the Doric peristyle outside.

The acanthus leaf was treated timidly at first, a simple applied motif, the leaves arranged in a single row of modest height around the central calathus that formed the body of the capital; in the hands of Scopas and the artists at Epidaurus it sprouted luxuriantly, arranged in two superimposed tiers from which escape twisted stalks that are surmounted by a curled leaf or calyx continuing into the volutes that supported the four projecting angles of the abacus. Early in the Hellenistic period the Corinthian capital assumed its definitive form on the Olympieion of Athens, for the last void of the capital was filled by decorative volutes on the axes, and these were crowned by a convolvulus flower nestled in the central depression of the abacus.

Hellenistic architecture had at its disposal a rich repertory of forms, much more varied than those it had inherited. But its inventiveness did not stop there; to satisfy the new requirements of architectural composition it perfected two other elements which the Classical age had known but deliberately left unstressed, namely, the engaged orders and the vault.

Since the end of the sixth century architects had used the half column engaged with the end of a wall (Temple of Athena, Paestum) or the column associated with a wall (especially where closures or interior balustrades were required: Temple of Athena Aphaia at Aegina, Temple of Zeus at Olympia), but the motif remained discreet, restricted to interior use. During the fifth century there were isolated attempts to develop special orders, such as the half columns and telamones of the great Temple of Zeus at Acragas, but

223. Athens, monument of Lysicrates.

*224-226. Syracuse, moats and
subterranean passages in fortifications
of Euryale Castle.*

in style and proportions it could not exert much influence. The engaged order, more decorative than structural, first entered upon an independent existence with the transformation of the interior hall; eventually it became an exterior element as well, and the principal theme of certain facades. Behind the Classical peristyles of the temples at Bassae and Tegea we have seen the role of engaged columns and pillars in the interior decoration: against cella walls displaying the Classical bond, with its strict regularity of alternate staggered and carefully centered joints, independent decoration of half columns was applied with no true architectonic function, though they supported sculptured friezes—with figures at Bassae, and with plant motifs at Tegea, where Corinthian half columns were surmounted by Ionic pilasters.

This theme of an applied order, distinct from the structural elements, marked a break with the great Classical tradition of form inseparable from function, but it belonged to a new trend that was assured of quick success and a tremendous future, for it became fundamental to Hellenistic and Roman architecture.

First seen in the scene structures associated with the Hellenistic theater, the engaged style spread rapidly to the facades of funerary monuments and then to the great decorative gateways within city walls. The style suited the rather theatrical taste in architecture of the Hellenistic princes. Often arranged in two stories, one Ionic or Doric, the other Ionic or Corinthian, the half columns or pillars projected from the walls that filled the bays on either side of arches and passageways. A gate in the walls of Thasos was built in this style at the end of the fourth century, and heralds the richer and more dynamic forms of the great Roman gate to the south agora at Miletus, abutting one of the back walls of one of the stoas.

The Macedonian tombs, such as the fine facade of that at Leucadia, exploit the same theme, often enhanced by painted decoration. This introduces one of the most important aspects of Hellenistic architecture: its pictorial effects and its close connections with painting. If the decorative mural painting of later periods was able to make such free use of huge architectural compositions, it was because architecture itself had called upon painting to accentuate the decorative values of its facades and interiors. The resulting experiments in effects of light and shade exerted a reciprocal influence on proportions: the spans of colonnades were widened, the supports heightened. Hermogenes adopted the so-called eustyle rhythm, the space between the columns equaling two and one-quarter column diameters, the height of the column being nine and one-half diameters; even more open was the diastyle rhythm, the column spacing equaling three diameters; as for the araeostyle (spacing at three and one-half diameters), according to Vitruvius it was unusable unless the entablature were of wood, since the span was too great for stone.

Effects of shadow and relief were enhanced on the engaged orders by applications of stucco and paint. On the facade of the tomb at Leucadia (early

229, 230. *Pergamum, lower city,*
vaulted stairway to first terrace.

231. *Locri, terra cotta model of*
fountain-sanctuary. Reggio Calabria,
National Museum.

232. *Priene, reconstruction of gate to*
agora (from Schede, 1964).

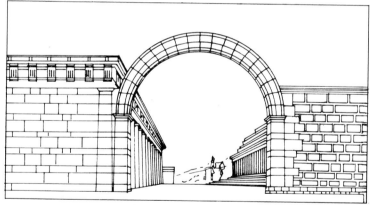

233. Sardis, Ionic capital of Temple
of Artemis Cybele.
234. Sardis, column base of east
portico, Temple of Artemis Cybele.

third century) the Ionic upper order was picked out with lines of dark red paint which defined the shafts and put them into relief. There were also false windows in paint, and the decorative frieze, between the two levels, was of painted stucco. The refinements of perspective are better understood; the play of shadow and the opposition of lighted zones have been systematically exploited in the mural decoration, which opened onto an imaginary architectural composition.

Finally, the arch and the vault were accepted definitively into the Hellenistic repertory. Mediterranean architecture had always employed the corbeled vault, as splendidly exemplified in the great Mycenaean tholoi. The tradition was not lost by the architects of Archaic Greece, who used it for tombs and aqueducts. But the bonded keystone arch does not appear until the fourth century, when it is superbly handled in the gateways of certain city walls; for examples, there are the Porta Rosa of the city of Velia, the ancient Phocian colony south of Paestum; the gates of Oeniadae in Acarnania; the subterranean passages of the theater at Alinda; and the vaulted tomb of Labranda in Caria. The Macedonian tombs of the late fourth and early third centuries offer fine illustrations of hemispherical vaults. The painted facade of the great tomb at Leucadia conceals a spacious hall covered by a vault, which is separate from the lower vault of the funerary chamber.

The Greeks had limited their use of the vault to subterranean buildings, where the structure had to resist powerful external thrusts. Its full significance stands revealed in the Nekyomanteion (oracle sanctuary) of Epirus, recently discovered in western Acarnania. The outer rooms of the sanctuary, built of rustic polygonal blocks whose deep joints vigorously set off the roughness of the picked faces, have linteled doors and the ceilings are flat-arched. The inner room was reserved for oracular consultation in the necromantic rites, and covered by a hemispherical vault reinforced by a series of overlapping arches in the walls.

Hellenistic architecture quickly took advantage of the possibilities of the arch, particularly in the construction of monumental gateways. At Priene, the eastern gate of the agora was enlarged this way in the second century. Thasos followed suit a century later. The theater of the Letoön at Xanthos offers one of the first examples of the vaulted opening with exterior decoration of pilasters and a pediment. The vault and vaulted stairways and exedrae are known to have been used by the architects of Pergamum.

The Buildings

A few examples of major buildings will suffice to illustrate the architectural forms at the disposal of the Hellenistic architect. Two great Ionic temples at Sardis and Didyma best expressed the broad trends in religious architecture of the period without breaking totally with the permanent elements of the Ionic order; the new Artemision of Ephesus, so often cited, adhered too closely to the Archaic model.

235. *Sardis, interior view toward*
east facade, Temple of Artemis Cybele.

The remains of the Temple of Artemis Cybele at Sardis, including the walls of the opisthodomos and a few of the east peristyle columns near it, still sprout from the wild Lydian landscape on the banks of the Pactolus River, where once was the famous capital of Croesus, whose very name has become a symbol of wealth. Several phases of construction have been distinguished, linked with different uses of the temple: in Roman times the west cella was reserved for Artemis, whereas the east hall was devoted to the cult of Faustina.

The sanctuary at Sardis originated with an altar erected at the edge of a level area. In the third century it was decided to build a huge peripteral edifice that would enclose this area within its dipteral plan. At that time only the naos was completed, consisting of a long cella divided into three aisles by two rows of six Ionic columns; the pronaos, deep like those of the Archaic temples at Ephesus and Samos, was originally adorned by two rows of three columns. A handsome capital from the interior order reveals the drift of the Ionic style away from the sober lines of the capitals inside the Propylaea at Athens. The Ionic peristyle was erected only a century later, but the design is transformed by the example of the Temple of Artemis at Magnesia on the Maeander, then being built by Hermogenes. The inner row of peristyle columns was suppressed to form a wide gallery (28 feet 9 inches) which set off the volume of the inner building.

The Temple of Apollo at Didyma remains the most grandiose example of religious architecture of this period and it also provides a virtual repertory for the forms devised and exploited by later centuries. It replaced an Archaic temple, a few traces of which have been found, but the architects Paeonius of Ephesus and Daphnis of Miletus, who supervised the reconstruction about 300 B.C., produced a most original design. Outwardly it appeared to be a large conventional dipteral Ionic temple, the tall cella surrounded by a double row of columns; the ten columns of the facade rose above a high crepidoma of seven steps, doubled to fourteen steps in the center along the width of the entrance stair. Columns sixty feet high were spaced apart 18 Ionian feet (17 feet 6 inches); the nine-foot square based on half of that column spacing was used as a module throughout the structure.

This sumptuous facade gave access to a deep twelve-column vestibule, the dodecastyle, four columns wide and three deep, and famous for their rich decoration. The bases present great variety: some have the Classical Attic profile of torus-scotiatorus; others remained in the Asian tradition derived from the bases of the Heraion at Samos, with layers of concave moldings, or smooth convex astragals crowning or crowned by a single torus. The square plinths with nine-foot sides are ever-present reminders of the underlying module, but the base moldings are sometimes replaced by an octagonal set of panels, framed by flat moldings and bearing motifs in low relief: rinceaux variously unrolled, marine animals or dragons, palmettes unfurled, spiral scrolls; the toruses are sometimes grooved, sometimes decorated with interlace or overlapping leaves. The decorative motifs on

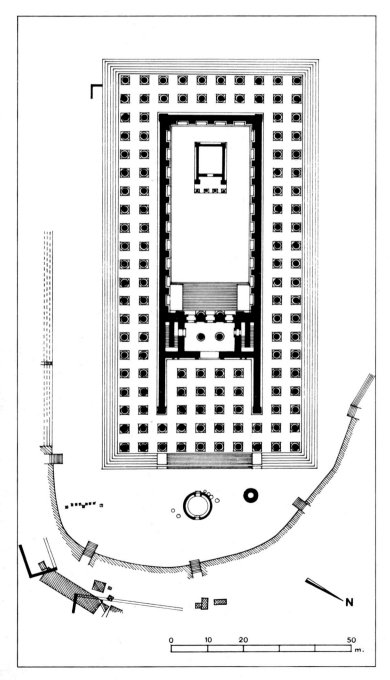

the toruses pass over to the comparable moldings along the base of the Ionic wall. The capitals express the same resourceful spirit of decoration: on the capitals of the angle columns, the volutes are capped by griffins' heads; beneath the gallery, some capitals bear the heads of Zeus, Apollo, Artemis, or Leto. Finally, the smooth architrave was crowned by a sculptured frieze of rinceaux and pilasters.

From this lavishly decorated pronaos were three openings with different uses. In the center, where one would expect the cella doors, there was a huge opening (18 feet wide, 46 feet high) made inaccessible by a sill over five feet higher than the pavement of the dodecastyle. No one could enter by this door: rather it was the "sacred doorway," having a special function emphasized by the enormous monoliths of its jambs and lintel, and from it were probably delivered the answers to the oracular consultations performed inside.

The two openings on either side of this tribunal gave access to sloping barrel-vaulted passages whose construction displays remarkable technical skill; these passages led down to the interior court that replaced the traditional cella. Huge (177 by 72 feet), and boldly structured by the high surrounding walls (height over 80 feet), the cella enclosed the primitive natural attributes of the oracle: the site of the spring, the laurel bush, and the adyton. The latter, in the form of an Ionic shrine or *naiskos,* sheltered the cult statue, and was situated at the west end of the court; from the east end a majestic flight of twenty-four steps, between the mouths of the two subterranean passages, led to the so-called labyrinth hall, on a level with the great "doorway" that dominated the twelve-columned pronaos.

The architects and sculptors of Didyma, the details of whose work is preserved in numerous inscriptions recording the costs of construction, displayed flexibility and skill in adapting every decorative resource to a project broadly conceived on a scale that far surpassed the Greek norm. In the second and first centuries B.C., and even later during Imperial times, decorators dipped into the repertory at Didyma and drew from its riches numerous motifs considered characteristic of later architectures; whether these systems originated in the western or the eastern Mediterranean world, many details were modeled upon the decoration of the temple of Didyma, such as carved rinceaux, decorative friezes with vegetable motifs, historiated capitals, the pilasters of the interior court, and decorated panels used on column bases.

There is another aspect of Hellenistic architecture that we must consider, namely, its new aesthetic approach based on a system of mathematical relations and proportions. This bears the imprint of Hermogenes from Priene or Alabanda, the great theoretician of the period, whose work exerted a strong influence on Vitruvius. His theories and aesthetic concerns are embodied in the buildings that he designed at Magnesia on the Meander River.

To lighten the complex plans of Archaic and Classical Ionia, Hermogenes

suppressed the inner row of columns in the peristyle of dipteral temple plans, while preserving the volumes and exterior proportions. Vitruvius has given Hermogenes' definition of this pseudo-dipteral design (*De architectura,* III, ii, 6): "The *pseudodipteros* is so planned that there are eight columns both in front and at the back, and fifteen on each side, including the angle columns. But the walls of the cella are to face the four middle columns in front and at the back. Thus there will be a space all around, from the walls to the outside rows of the columns, of two intercolumniations and the thickness of one column. There is no example of this at Rome; but there is at Magnesia the temple of Diana built by Hermogenes of Alabanda..." In elevations Hermogenes intended to apply the same principles, with the object of freeing the interior volumes and enlarging the voids and open spaces, and thus he classified the different kinds of colonnades by their ratio of intercolumniation to column diameter, from the pycnostyle colonnade, the most crowded, to the araeostyle, with too few columns to support a stone entablature.

In buildings at Magnesia we can see the application of Hermogenes' principles, and the facade of the Temple of Zeus Sosipolis, which he built on the agora of Magnesia, exactly reproduces his scheme. The deep pronaos, as large as the cella, is preceded by a tetrastyle porch; the opisthodomos, half the size of the pronaos, has two columns in antis; the ratio of these three spaces is 2:2:1, and the square of the pronaos (21 by 21 feet) reappears in the facade (column height and distance between lateral axes, 21 feet each);

the proportions of the order are eustyle, the height of the columns corresponding to nine and one-half times the diameter (26 inches) and the intercolumniation to two and one-quarter diameters.

Shortly after the temple was built, the agora was enclosed by a system of stoas associated with the neighboring sanctuary of Artemis Leukophryne, located on that site before the order of a regular city plan was imposed. As Vitruvius points out, the Temple of Artemis is also a strict example of the pseudo-dipteral plan. The column spacing constitutes the module on which the design of the temple was based. The width of the pteron is equal to two modules. The naos, like the cella, is four modules deep, whereas the opisthodomos has only half that depth; this gives the same ratio (2:2:1) as in the Temple of Zeus. The entablatures of both temples include all the traditional Ionic elements: architrave, and frieze with dentils. In the tympanum of the pediment there is a large opening above the middle bay, which is slightly wider than the others, and two smaller openings are symmetrically disposed on the axes of the second and sixth bays. The insistence on slender proportions and lightened columns made it necessary to lighten the entablature and pediment; moreover the interior layout, with two rows of very close-set columns, required illumination appropriate to the nature of the rites and ceremonies of the cult.

Thus Hermogenes emerges as the great theoretician of Hellenistic architecture, whose principles and completed buildings exerted a distant influence on the proportions of the Ionic order into Imperial Roman times.

Let us bring to a close these observations on buildings of the Hellenistic period with a group of works that illustrate one of its most important attributes, its relationship with sculpture.

Of course, temples and funerary monuments since Archaic times had had sculptured decorations, first in relief, later in the round. It was placed in favored positions and associated with particular parts of the structure. There were precise rules controlling the use and development of monumental sculpture. The korai and caryatids in the Ionic treasuries at Delphi and the Erechtheion on the Athenian acropolis supported an entablature, and were closely linked with the architecture because of their structural functions; in the Olympieion at Acragas, the telamones attached to the walls rhythmically punctuated each bay formed by the Doric half columns, themselves integral with the masonry.

The integration of sculptural groups and architecture began early in the fourth century with the Nereid Monument at Xanthos, and, a little later, the Mausoleum at Halicarnassus. Friezes proliferated, and tall podiums supported not only the tomb chamber, but statues of gods or heroes; these sometimes stood between the columns, as at Xanthos, introducing a movement and rhythm that seemed to break the strict architectural composition. The origins of these characteristics can be found in monuments on the Lycian acropolis; in the fifth century they belonged to the eastern

244. Priene, plan of Temple of
Athena Polias (from Bervé-Gruben,
1962).

246. Magnesia, front elevation of
Altar of Artemis (from Gerkan,
1929).

245. Magnesia, plan of Temple of
Artemis (from Lawrence, 1957).

247. Magnesia, plan of Altar of
Artemis (from Gerkan, 1929).

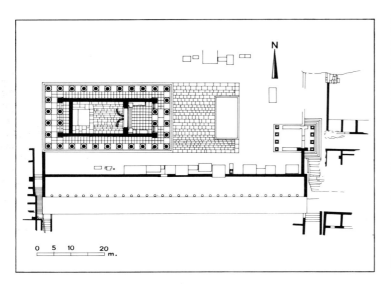

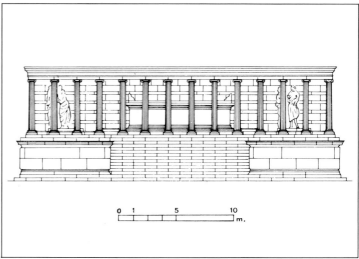

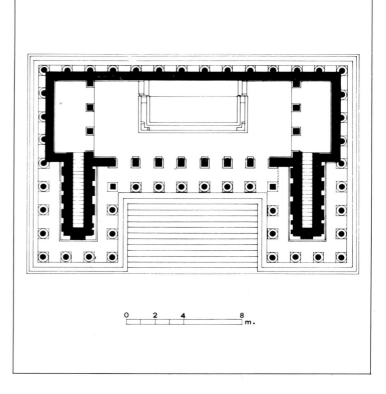

248. *Pergamum, restoration of Great Altar of Zeus. Berlin, Pergamum Museum.*

249. *Sarcophagus of the Mourning Women. Istanbul, Archaeological Museum.*

traditions which, as in Egypt, had since the second millennium more readily associated divine or royal effigies with the interior or exterior colonnades of religious buildings. The Lycian princes, like the satraps of Caria, were sympathetic to the eastern and the indigenous traditions, while adapting them to the Hellenic decorations that they commissioned from Greek artists.

It is important to think of the silhouette of the Lycian and Carian monuments, rising on massive podia crowned by one or two friezes and an Ionic-type cornice enriched with two or three rows of superimposed egg-and-tongue ornament. The effigies, divine or heroic, were distributed at both Halicarnassus and Xanthos along the top of the podium, either isolated or in association with the colonnades of the tomb chambers. The same principle was later applied in the great monumental altars of Pergamum, Priene, and Magnesia during the third and second centuries.

The most famous of these altars is the one dedicated by the Attalids to Zeus and Athena, perhaps even to all the gods of the city, on one of the terraces of the acropolis at Pergamum. The plan was in the tradition of Ionian altars, the sacrificial slab placed on a tall stepped base with lateral salients. Eumenes II, at the beginning of the second century, transformed this traditional scheme into a sumptuous monumental ensemble whose architectural forms and sculptural motifs were closely associated. The whole rested on a five-step crepidoma inscribed in a square (120 by 113 feet); from this a majestic flight of steps led up to the central platform, framed by two projecting wings; the podium consisted of a lower course of smooth orthostats whose crowning molding formed the base of a mighty frieze celebrating the legendary struggles of the gods and giants. This frieze, seven and one-half feet tall and unfolding over a length of four hundred feet, was one of the finest achievements of the sculptors of Pergamum, indeed of the entire Hellenistic period. Above the frieze ran a decorated cornice, completing the podium as well. On the podium, walls fronted by an Ionic colonnade enclosed the altar slab on north, south, and east, the west side being occupied by the monumental stairway. Along the inner face of this wall ran another smaller frieze illustrating the story of Telephus. Finally, in the bays overlooking the stairway stood statues of the gods or of allegorical figures.

The same plan and the same decorative themes were used for the altars at Priene and Magnesia, though less lavishly and on a smaller scale. In each case the platform bearing the altar slab was on top of a crepidoma with several steps and there were two projecting wings, the whole surrounded by an Ionic colonnade. The podium did not have a frieze, but a series of figures carved in high relief occupied the bays of the colonnade on the facade and along the short sides.

In these compositions one can discern the origins of the theme which in later centuries took the form of niches integrated with the architectural design framed by columns and pediments; these niches decorated the tall facades of theater buildings, nymphaea, and palaces in Roman architecture.

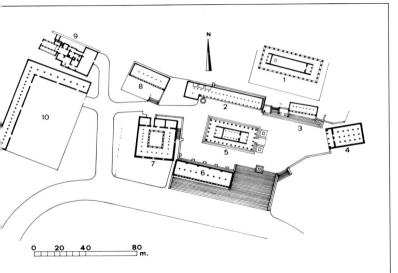

0 20 40   80
m.

1. Temple of Hera, before 600 B.C. / 2, 3, 8. Doric stoa, Archaic period / 4. Hypostyle hall, similar to Telesterion / 5. Temple of Hera II, end of 4th century B.C. / 6. Stoa / 7. Ancient banquet house / 9. Roman baths / 10. Gymnasium

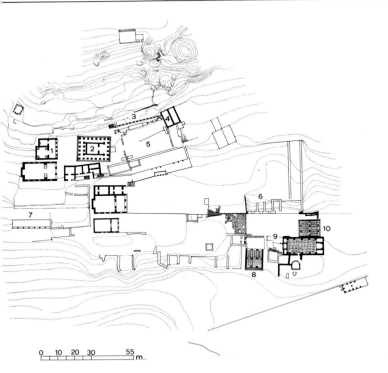

0 10 20 30   55
m.

1. West terrace of temple / 2. Temple of Zeus / 3. North stoa / 4. East house / 5. East terrace of temple / 6. Palace (?) / 7. West stoa / 8. South propylon / 9. Doric house / 10. East propylon

THE ORGANIZATION OF SPACE AND HELLENISTIC CITY-PLANNING

The design of monumental ensembles and their relationship to the surrounding space underwent a fundamental change at the beginning of the Hellenistic period. In the history of Greek architecture this transformation was perhaps the greatest Hellenistic innovation. For the buildings of the Archaic and Classical sanctuaries and agoras had been designed according to their specific function and individual character; space was organized around them freely, and it accommodated, without much regularity, the secondary structures. Whenever urban policy required a more rigid frame, architectural space was still treated openly, in direct relation to the surrounding zones.

Many factors combined to create a new conception of the architectural ensemble: the political evolution, that substituted the centralizing tendencies and ostentation of the Hellenistic princes for the diverse and sometimes divergent forms of monumental expression preferred by the Greek cities; the transformation of aesthetic interests toward plastic and pictorial effects, as well as monumentality; and the corresponding influence of the arts of painting and sculpture. Buildings lost their autonomy, becoming integrated with the surrounding structures that enclosed and unified them; the monumental masses thus became dependent, one and all, upon a space sharply defined and rigorously delimited; esplanades and squares were surrounded by porticoes, cutting off an area in which the interior was treated as a single uniform design. Out of this was created an architectural landscape, all of the elements interdependent and organized according to their plastic or pictorial effects; thus the door was opened to the great laws of axial planning and symmetrical ponderation which entered discreetly at first, later to be asserted with ever-increasing boldness.

This evolution was facilitated by two methods that seem to be contradictory, but in reality acted in the same direction. One was the development of city plans based on a rectangular grid, the space blocked out in well-defined zones contained by long colonnades; the other was the success of terrace composition, a type of planning that proceeds with precise, compact groupings unrelated to one another.

The latter trend, the more innovative of the two, deserves particular attention. The sanctuary of Apollo at Delphi, that of Hera on the edge of the plain of Argos, and other less well-known sites in the Peloponnesus prove that Greek architects since Archaic times had taken advantage of the different levels of the terrain to enhance their buildings. Each was treated independently, however, with no attempt to establish a relationship between masses or volumes.

In the course of the fourth century a new element was introduced by the architects who worked for the satraps of Caria—for Mausolus at Halicarnassus, for his brother Idrieus in the sanctuaries at Labranda and Amyzon, and for his sister Adda in her capital of Alinda. Vitruvius'

253. *Lindos (Rhodes), grand staircase to upper terrace of acropolis.*

254. *Lindos (Rhodes), great portico at foot of grand staircase, lower terrace of acropolis.*

255. *Lindos (Rhodes), cella of Temple of Athena, on upper terrace.*

description of the city of Halicarnassus; the excavations at Labranda and Amyzon; and the remains at Alinda—each of these points to a system of great terraces, boldly defined by handsome retaining walls and linked by flights of stairs crowned by propylaea. On these terraces the buildings are placed and grouped with the clear intention to treat them as parts of an ensemble; though relatively small, they occupy privileged positions that integrate the buildings with the lines of the artificial landscape. The Greek architects were here inspired more by Achaemenid than by Hellenic tradition, and more by royal architecture than by that of the democratic cities.

The terraces also made use of great porticoes, the lower level acting as a retaining wall and housing basement service quarters, the upper story enlarging the terrace while limiting it. The large portico of the agora at Alinda was one of the splendid models that herald the Pergamenian porticoes.

The development of this terrace architecture is illustrated by two great sanctuaries, that of Athena at Lindos, on Rhodes, and the Asclepieion of Kos. Lindos is especially instructive because the modeling of the successive terraces with the aid of porticoes, colonnades, and interlocking stairways was carried out in successive stages, so that one can recognize the processes used by the architects to impose a unity that is sometimes artificial. The holy place dedicated to Athena Lindia goes back to Archaic times, and the first temple was built on the highest terrace at the edge of the cliff, to be associated, it seems, with the sacred grotto hollowed out beneath. This ritual siting remained unaffected by later quests for symmetry.

The first plan for developing the upper terrace was prepared early in the third century, according to the new concepts of that epoch: a huge propylon marks the entrance to the sanctuary, with five doorways pierced in the central wall; to these corresponds a portico with a ten-column facade having at each end, following the example of Mnesicles' Propylaea, a prostyle bastion with four columns enclosing the passageway. The altar is aligned with the entrance and the court is bordered by porticoes on the north, east, and west sides. At the end of the same century or the beginning of the second, the lower terrace was integrated with the sanctuary and to it was assigned the role of monumental gateway: a grand staircase was broadly laid out in front of the propylon, and the foot of the terrace was developed as a large colonnade 225 feet wide, also having projecting wings. Where it met the grand staircase the portico had to be interrupted, and only the colonnade continued; across the opening was drawn the long curtain of Doric columns with no serious attempt at solving the problem of continuity. Thus the same themes were repeated at each level, at the price of certain anomalies but with the result that the contours and elevations of the successive terraces were perfectly modeled within an all-encompassing architectural structure.

A comparable and no less grandiose evolution may be traced in the

258. *Pergamum, plan of acropolis*
(from Bervé-Gruben, 1962).

259. *Pergamum, model of acropolis.*
Berlin, Pergamum Museum.

260. *Pergamum, Acropolis,*
foundations of Palace of Eumenes II,
from northwest.

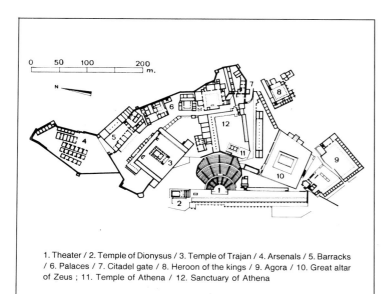

1. Theater / 2. Temple of Dionysus / 3. Temple of Trajan / 4. Arsenals / 5. Barracks
/ 6. Palaces / 7. Citadel gate / 8. Heroon of the kings / 9. Agora / 10. Great altar
of Zeus ; 11. Temple of Athena / 12. Sanctuary of Athena

development of the sanctuary of Asclepius on Kos. It was located on the slopes of the hills forming the southern boundary of the plain where stood the city and port of Kos; this spot, like all the Asclepieia, was made holy by the presence of natural springs welling from the hillside. The first modest Ionic temple (Temple C) was built on an intermediate terrace, where an altar had been erected at the beginning of the fourth century; the surviving portions of the temple were part of a rebuilding program carried out in the second century in accordance with Hermogenes' recommendations. At the beginning of the second century a small portico and what may have been a square abaton (reclining house) were added to complete the still rudimentary installation; the buildings were arranged in the old manner, placed without thought for anything but cult practices, and there is no evidence of conscious architectural grouping.

The main monumental building program appears to have been started about the middle of the second century. A relatively level stretch at the foot of the hill was treated as a huge entrance court; the uppermost terrace became the site of a new sanctuary, associated with the old intermediate terrace but designed according to quite different principles, with axial symmetry an overriding concern. The forecourt, which measured 307 by 155 feet, was surrounded on the north, east, and west sides by a Doric colonnade. A massive retaining wall closed off the south side and incorporated the two springs that were the object of the primitive cult; the upper level of the wall regularized the extent of the original terrace. The

dispersion of the early buildings and the irregularity of the terrace prevented the use of axial symmetry, but where possible the principle was observed. Thus, the forecourt at the bottom of the hill was entered through a propylon on the axis of the central portico, dividing it into two symmetrical parts with projecting wings. On the same axis was placed the first monumental stair leading to the middle terrace.

The organization of the uppermost terrace was also ruled by the concept of axial symmetry. A U-shaped portico, corresponding to the forecourt portico but open to the north, enclosed the terrace on three sides. On the axis was the stairway linking the two upper terraces and the great Doric peripteral Temple of Asclepius, a larger replica of the god's temple at Epidaurus.

These two examples illustrate the dual preoccupation of Hellenistic architecture, that of composing a monumental ensemble of columns and masses interrelated with one another and mutually reinforced by the terrace system, and of arranging these ensembles along axial or symmetrical lines. Both intentions were completely alien to Classical Greek architecture, but their lesson was not lost, and the effect that these experiments had on early Roman architecture is well known. The sanctuary of Fortuna at Praeneste was a direct descendant of Hellenistic terrace architecture, adapted to an

263. Pergamum, middle city, east end
of Sanctuary of Demeter.

*264, 265. Pergamum, middle city,
Sanctuary of Demeter: section of south
stoa, temple, steps, and north stoa
(from Bervé-Gruben, 1962).*

*266. Pergamum, Acropolis Temple
of Dionysus.*

*267. Athens, agora, view from
northwest, toward Stoa of Attalus.*

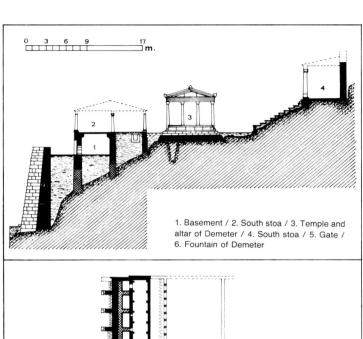

1. Basement / 2. South stoa / 3. Temple and
altar of Demeter / 4. South stoa / 5. Gate /
6. Fountain of Demeter

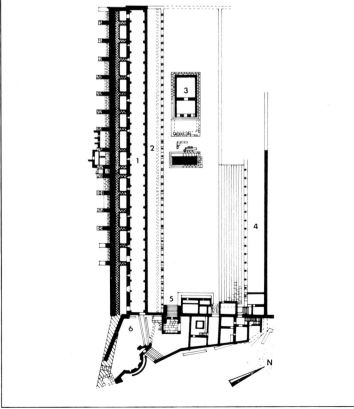

268. *Athens, agora, east facade of Temple of Hephaestus (Theseum).*
269. *Athens, agora, restoration of Stoa of Attalus.*

270. *Athens, agora, colonnade of Stoa of Attalus (in background, Temple of Hephaestus).*

Italic tradition that was itself predisposed in favor of axial symmetry.

The great movement of urbanism in the Hellenistic age adapted and transformed the principles evolved during the preceding period in accordance with the rules of the new aesthetics. The more effective disposition of monumental masses, the concern for space much more strictly delimited and organized, the imposition of architectural unity and closed contours, and the systematic use of long colonnades to accentuate the monumentality of dispersed urban architecture—all these were primary concerns in Hellenistic urbanism and found expression in the many new cities created by the expansionary policies of Hellenistic princes. Their wealth and ambition assured the best use of the techniques and forms that the architects had at their disposal—indeed, architecture was one part of their propaganda.

Among these masterworks, Pergamum and its acropolis offer an excellent example of a terraced urban architecture, the very irregularities of the terrain displaying the monumental masses to best advantage. Halfway up the acropolis, whose highest level is more than a thousand feet above sea level, the gymnasia received first attention, laid out on three terraces in a great curve formed by the city's main thoroughfare which hugs the twisting contours of the steep hillside. From the rising street, a porticoed fountain at its side, a staircase leads to the first terrace through a vaulted passage with two flights, their barrel vaults at right angles to one another and at different levels. From the first triangular esplanade, which formed the tip of the composition, one ascended stairs leading to the second terrace, whose longest side was bordered by a covered track one stadium in length (100 Greek feet; about 600 feet), its roof at the same height as the level of the upper terrace. This ensured the optimal aesthetic and functional relationship with the great gymnasia, which extended around a broad esplanade 600 by 150 feet. The view, as always at Pergamum, was toward the south, and the principal halls of the gymnasia backed into the north cliff. The ephebeion, with its odeum, or music theater, was linked with the facade portico by a group of four columns, and followed by several exercise rooms covered in Roman times with semidomes. The Hellenistic buildings were made of local stone, a dark volcanic andesite that blended with the countryside; all the porticoes were Doric. Rebuilding programs carried out during the Roman period made greater use of marble and introduced the more decorative Corinthian column.

To the northwest lay the sanctuary of Demeter, linked with the gymnasia by a small terrace that ran along both sides of the main street. Perched on a terrace oriented east and west, the sanctuary was especially dear to the Attalid rulers. When inaugurated by Philetairos, the founder of the dynasty, it consisted of a small temple and its altar, opposite the entrance. Against the north slope, along the eastern esplanade, was the altar, where tiers of steps were arranged for the faithful; these terminated toward the west in a simple portico accompanying the temple.

At the end of the third century Apollonia, wife of Attalus I, was

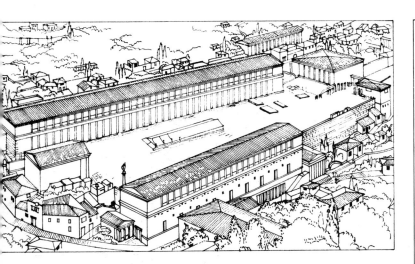

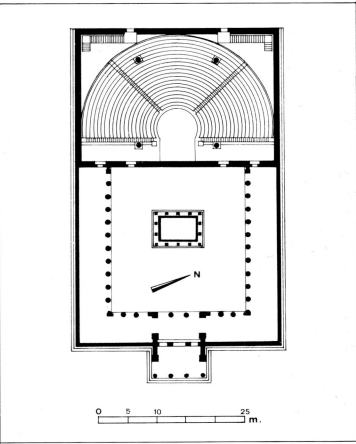

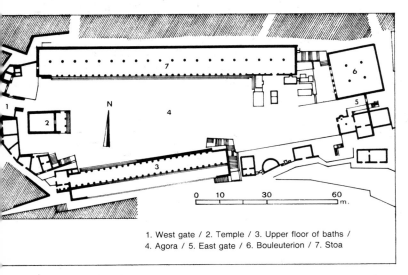

1. West gate / 2. Temple / 3. Upper floor of baths /
4. Agora / 5. East gate / 6. Bouleuterion / 7. Stoa

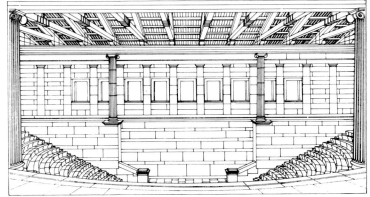

275. *Miletus, theater, from east.*

responsible for certain drastic changes that express with unusual clarity the extraordinary technical skill of the Pergamene architects. On the south, where the ground fell sharply toward the plain, the terrace was extended by building a monumental portico 280 feet long; its foundations were beyond and below the edge of the esplanade, in direct relationship with the steep terrain; an underground gallery was then constructed at the lower level, reached by a narrow path leading from the entrance to the sanctuary. At terrace level the south stoa, double-aisled and with two colonnades, provided a splendid open gallery for the view over the plain; on the west it turned to close off the sanctuary and join the north portico; this portico continued toward the east, above the tiers of steps, creating another gallery overlooking the south portico, to the plain and shore beyond.

We must mention that the lowest level, beneath the underground gallery, was reserved for basement service quarters. Here, in the third century, is the prototype of a long series of buildings combining porticoes and underground rooms which the architects of the Attalids were to export to the subject territories of the Pergamene dynasty, or its friends and allies—to Aegaea, Assos, and Pamphylia; their successors would later adopt it and, as the cryptoporticus system, make it an essential element of private and civic architecture in Roman cities. The Imperial age is rich in examples in all provinces, from the agora at Smyrna to the fora at Arles and at Conimbriga in Portugal.

One can only remark again, before leaving the subject of Pergamum, on the success of the Attalid architects in designing the acropolis. The theater was placed like the pivot of a fan of terraces at different levels, limited at the top by the arsenal and at the south extremity by the agora. Between these utilitarian installations the area to the east held the princely palaces, protected by walls and rocky cliffs, and the west was reserved for the gods with Athena at the center, her sanctuary dominated by the Temple of Trajan above it and the Great Altar of Zeus and Athena below it. To Attalus I and Eumenes II goes the glory for this splendid architectural composition, realized mainly during the last third of the third century and the first quarter of the fourth; what followed were continuations or finishing touches.

The influence of Pergamene architecture is linked with the political and historical conditions that marked the evolution of the Attalid kingdom. The Attalids were proud of their achievements, ambitious and desirous of being the true representatives of Hellenism in Asia Minor; with considerable resources at their disposal, they sent architects along with their ambassadors. The cities allied with Pergamum, and the venerable cities of Greece, such as Athens, as well as great sanctuaries such as those at Delphi and Delos, welcomed the teams of architects and masons dispatched by the Attalids. Later, their close understanding and cordial relations with Rome favored the spread of Pergamene art to the west, where the extent of its influence is well known. Imperial Rome learned much about composition from the architects and sculptors of Pergamum and borrowed extensively from their

repertory of forms and motifs.

But no account of architecture in the Hellenized and Romanized countries east and south of the Mediterranean would be complete without the monumental architecture of Miletus. Within a geometric framework more rigorously defined than the terraces of Pergamum, a taste for ensembles and for unified, organized monumental masses accompanied the expansion of the rectangular grid system. At Miletus, within the network laid out in the fifth century B.C., one follows the formation of enclosed structures. Colonnades were progressively substituted for the simple walls bounding the north agora, the Bouleuterion and its precincts, the adjoining sanctuary, and the gymnasia, and, finally, for the monumental street that formed the common axis along which these complexes were grouped. Porticoes gave better definition to the sides of the grid, and colonnades enclosed the main buildings according to the principles of axial symmetry.

It would be well to mention here, however sketchily, the architectural splendors at Alexandria, where Hellenistic techniques were combined with the sense of spaciousness and grandiosity inherent in the local tradition. The monumental zones were grouped together in the north, where they were dominated by Alexander's Pharos. The palaces, museums, and great sanctuaries such as the Serapeum appear to have made extensive use of long colonnades and porticoes to form broad squares within which the principal buildings were subsequently erected. Museum collections in Cairo and Alexandria show the taste for vigorous decoration, and the particular popularity of the Corinthian style. The great features of ancient Alexandria must be evoked in large Hellenistic and Roman cities of Cyrenaica and Libya. Certain details are also supplied by the Alexandrian landscape paintings at Pompeii, in which piers, column-decorated waterfronts, monumental arches, long porticoed streets, and formal facades recall the ruined cities of Asia Minor and Syria. How pleasant to stroll for a moment along the great avenue of Cyrene, past the gymnasia, the Caesareum, and the sanctuary of Zeus, and before the porticoes of the agora! One would find there, as at Perge and Side on the Mediterranean shore of Anatolia, or at Gerasa in the Syrian interior, long porticoed streets lined with shops, colorful and bustling with life; the closed symmetrical contours of great buildings would be now concealed, now splendidly revealed; beyond a propylon with its four or six columns the visitor would glimpse a monumental Ionic or Corinthian temple facade; broad colonnades unfolded to right and left in subtle harmonies of light and shade. This lavish repertory was available to the architects from east and west, and later to the architects who served the Roman emperors.

LIST OF PHOTOGRAPHIC CREDITS

Aurelio Amendola, Pistoia: 91, 96, 99, 101

Bruno Balestrini, Milan: I, VII, X, XII, XVI, XVII, XVIII, XXII, XXIII, XXIV

Federico Borromeo, Milan: V

British Museum, London: 79, 81

Foto Mairani, Milan: III

Fotocielo, Rome: 102, 192

Musée d'Archéologie, Marseilles: 159

Francesco Quadarella, Agrigento: 217

Ezio Quiresi, Cremona: 104, 207

Luisa Ricciarini, Milan: II, IV, VIII, IX, XIX, XX, XXI

Roberto Schezen/Ricciarini, Milan: VI, XI, XIII, XIV, XV

Soprintendenza alle Antichità, Reggio Calabria: 115, 231

Staatliche Museen, Berlin: 248, 259

CRETE AND MYCENAE

BOSSERT, H. Altkreta. 3rd ed. Berlin, 1937.

CHARBONNEAUX, J., JOLY, R. DEMARGNE, P. Études Crétoises; Fouilles de Mallia, vols. I and II. Paris, 1928–

DEMARGNE, P. Naissance de l'art grec. Paris, 1964.

EVANS, A. J. The Palace of Minos at Knossos, vols. I–VII. London, 1921–36.

GRAHAM, J. W. The Palaces of Crete. Princeton, 1962.

MARINATOS, S., and HIRMER, M. Crete and Mycenae. New York, 1960.

MATZ, F. Creta e la Grecia preistorica. Milan, 1963.

MYLONAS, G. E. Ancient Mycenae. Princeton, 1957.

PERNIER, L., and BANTI, L. Guida degli scavi italiani in Creta. Rome, 1967.

PLATON, N. La Crète et la Grèce primitive. Geneva, 1968.

TAYLOUR, W. I Micenei. Milan, 1966.

WACE, A. J. B. Mycenae. Princeton, 1969.

GREECE

General works:

BERVE, H., GRUBEN, G., and HIRMER, M. Greek Temples, Theatres, and Shrines. New York, 1962.

CHARBONNEAUX, J., MARTIN, R., and VILLARD, F. Grèce archaïque. Paris, 1968.

CHOISY, A. Histoire de l'architecture. 2 vols. Paris, 1929.

—— Grèce classique. Paris, 1969.

DINSMOOR, W. B. The Architecture of Ancient Greece. 3rd ed. London, 1950.

ESPONY, H. Fragments d'architecture d'après les relevées et restaurations des anciens pensionnaires de l'Académie de France à Rome. 2 vols. Paris, 1905.

GRUBEN, G. Die Tempel der Griechen. Munich, 1966.

LAWRENCE, A. W. Greek Architecture. Baltimore, 1957.

MARTENSSEN, R. D. The Idea of Space in Greek Architecture. 2nd ed. Johannesburg, 1964.

MARTIN, R. Monde grec, in series Architecture Universelle. Freiburg, 1966.

—— Manuel d'architecture grecque, I: Matériaux et techniques. Paris, 1965.

ORLANDOS, A. Les Matériaux de construction et la technique architecturale des Anciens Grecs. Paris, 1966.

PORTOGHESI, P., ed. Dizionario enciclopedico di architettura e urbanistica. Rome, 1968–69.

WEICKERT, C. Typen der archaischen Architektur in Griechenland und Kleinasien. Augsburg, 1929.

City planning:

CASTAGNOLI, F. Ippodamo di Mileto e l'urbanistica a pianta ortogonale. Rome, 1956.

DI VITA, A. "La stoa nel temenos del tempio C e lo sviluppo programmato di Selinunte," in Palladio, 1967, pp. 1–60.

GIULIANO, A. Urbanistica delle città greche. Milan, 1966.

MARTIN, R. L'Urbanisme dans la Grèce antique. Paris, 1956.

WYCHERLEY, R. E. How the Greeks Built Cities, 2nd ed. London, 1962.

Special studies:

ADRIANI, A., BONACASA, N., et al. Himera I. Rome, 1970.

AKERSTRÖM, A. Die Architektonischen Terrakotten Kleinasiens. Lund, 1966.

ANTI, C. Teatri greci arcaici. Padua, 1967.

AUBERSON, P. Eretria, I: Temple d'Apollon Daphnéphoros. Bern, 1968.

BERGQUIST, B. The Archaic Greek Temenos. Lund, 1967.

BOERSMA, J. S. Athenian Building Policy from 561/560 to 405/404 B.C. Groningen, 1970.

BOURAS, C. The Restoration of the Stoa of Brauron: Architectural Problems. Athens, 1967 (in Greek).

BÜSING, H. Die Griechische Halbsäule. Wiesbaden, 1970.

BUTLER, H. C. Sardis II, Architecture. I: The Temple of Artemis. Leyden, 1925.

DEMARGNE, P., and COUPEL, P. Fouilles de Xanthos, III: Le Monument des Néréides, l'Architecture. Paris, 1969.

GABRICI, E. "Per la storia dell'architettura dorica in Sicilia," in Estratto dai Monumenti Antichi, R. Acc. dei Lincei, Rome, 1935 and 1936.

GERKAN, A. VON. Der Altar des Artemistempels in Magnesia am Mäander. Berlin, 1929.

—— and MÜLLER-WIENER, M. Das Theater von Epidauros. Stuttgart, 1961.

GINOUVÈS, R. Balaneutikè: Recherches sur le bain dans l'antiquité grecque. Paris, 1962.

HILL, B. H., and KAUFMANN, C. H. The Temple of Zeus at Nemea. Princeton, 1966.

KLEINER, G. Die Ruinen von Milet. Berlin, 1968.

KOLDEWEY, R., and PUCHSTEIN, O. Die griechische Tempel in Unteritalien und Sizilien. Berlin, 1899.

LEHMANN, K. Samothrace, 4–1: The Hall of Votive Gifts. New York, 1962; 4–2: The Altar Court. New York, 1964; 4–3: The Hieron. New York, 1969.

MAIER, F. G. Griechische Mauerbauinschriften. Heidelberg, 1959.

MANSEL, A. M. Die Ruinen von Side. Berlin, 1963.

MANSUELLI, G. A. Architettura e città. Bologna, 1970.

MILTNER, F. Ephesos: Stadt der Artemis und des Johannes. Vienna, 1958.

NOVICKA, M. La Maison privée dans l'Égypte Ptolémaïque. Warsaw, 1969.

RIDER, B. C. Ancient Greek Houses. rev. ed. Chicago, 1964.

ROUX, G. L'Architecture de l'Argolide au IVe et IIIe siècles avant J. C. Paris, 1961.

—— Delphi. Munich, 1972.

SCHEDE, M. Die Ruinen von Priene. 2nd ed. Berlin, 1964.

SHOE, L. T. Profiles of Greek Mouldings, 2 vols. Cambridge, Mass., 1936.

—— Profiles of Western Greek Mouldings. Rome, 1952.

VALLET, G., and VILLARD, F. Megara Hyblaea, IV: Le Temple du IVe siècle. Paris, 1966.

VALOIS, R. L'Architecture hellénique et hellénistique à Délos, 2 vols. Paris, 1966 and 1964.

WESENBERG, B. Kapitelle und Basen. Düsseldorf, 1971.

WESTHOLM, A. "Labraunda, Swedish Excavations and Researches, I, 2: The Architecture of the Hieron," in Acta instituti Atheniensis regni Sueciae, vol. no. 2, Lund, 1963.

WINTER, F. Greek Fortifications. London, 1971.

YAVIS, C. G. Greek Altars: Origins and Typology. St. Louis, Mo., 1949.

ZANCANI-MONTUORO, P., and ZANOTTI-BIANCO, U. Heraion alla foce del Sele. Rome, 1951.

For individual buildings and their characteristics consult the collections and periodical publications devoted to particular localities: Athens, Corinth, Delos, Delphi, Labranda, Miletus, Olympia, Pergamum, Sardis, Thasos.